Safe C++

Vladimir Kushnir

Beijing · Cambridge · Farnham · Köln · Sebastopol · Tokyo

Safe C++

by Vladimir Kushnir

Published by O'Reilly Media, Inc., 1005 Gravenstein Highway North, Sebastopol, CA 95472.

O'Reilly books may be purchased for educational, business, or sales promotional use. Online editions are also available for most titles (*http://my.safaribooksonline.com*). For more information, contact our corporate/institutional sales department: (800) 998-9938 or *corporate@oreilly.com*.

Editors: Andy Oram and Mike Hendrickson	**Indexer:** BIM Publishing Services
Production Editor: Iris Febres	**Cover Designer:** Karen Montgomery
Copyeditor: Emily Quill	**Interior Designer:** David Futato
Proofreader: BIM Publishing Services	**Illustrator:** Robert Romano

June 2012:   First Edition.

Revision History for the First Edition:
    2012-05-25   First release
See *http://oreilly.com/catalog/errata.csp?isbn=9781449320935* for release details.

ISBN: 978-1-449-32093-5

[LSI]

1337956721

To Daria and Misha

Table of Contents

Part III.   The Joy of Bug Hunting: From Testing to Debugging to Production

Preface

Astute readers such as yourself may be wondering whether the title of this book, *Safe C++*, presumes that the C++ programming language is somehow unsafe. Good catch! That is indeed the presumption. The C++ language allows programmers to make all kinds of mistakes, such as accessing memory beyond the bounds of an allocated array, or reading memory that was never initialized, or allocating memory and forgetting to deallocate it. In short, there are a great many ways to shoot yourself in the foot while programming in C++, and everything will proceed happily along until the program abruptly crashes, or produces an unreasonable result, or does something that in computer literature is referred to as "unpredictable behavior." So yes, in this sense, the C++ language is inherently unsafe.

This book discusses some of the most common mistakes made by us, the programmers, in C++ code, and offers recipes for avoiding them. The C++ community has developed many good programming practices over the years. In writing this book I have collected a number of these, slightly modified some, and added a few, and I hope that this collection of rules formulated as one bug-hunting strategy is larger than the sum of its parts.

The undeniable truth is that any program significantly more complex than "Hello, World" will contain some number of errors, also affectionately called "bugs." The Great Question of Programming is how we can reduce the number of bugs without slowing the process of programming to a halt. To start with, we need to answer the following question: just who is supposed to catch these bugs?

There are four participants in the life of the software program (Figure P-1):

1. The programmer
2. The compiler (such as g++ under Unix/Linux, Microsoft Visual Studio under Windows, and XCode under Mac OS X)
3. The runtime code of the application
4. The user of the program

Of course, we don't want the user to see the bugs or even know about their existence, so we are left with participants 1 through 3. Like the user, programmer is human, and humans can get tired, sleepy, hungry, distracted by colleagues asking questions or by

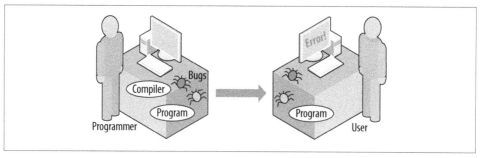

Figure P-1. Four participants (buggy version)

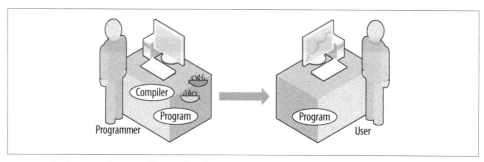

Figure P-2. Four participants (happy/less buggy version)

phone calls from family members or a mechanic working on their car, and so on. In short, humans make mistakes, the programmer is human, and therefore the programmer makes mistakes, a.k.a. bugs. In comparison, participants 2 and 3—the compiler and the executable code—have some advantages: they do not get tired, sleepy, depressed, or burned out, and do not attend meetings or take vacations or lunch breaks. They just execute instructions and usually are very good at doing it.

Considering our resources we have to deal with—the programmer on the one hand, and the compiler and program on the other—we can adopt one of two strategies to reduce the number of bugs:

Choice Number 1: Convince the programmer not to make mistakes. Look him in the eyes, threaten to subtract $10 from his bonus for each bug, or otherwise stress him out in the hopes to improve his productivity. For example, tell him something like this: "Every time you allocate memory, do not forget to de-allocate it! Or else!"

Choice Number 2: Organize the whole process of programming and testing based on a realistic assumption that even with the best intentions and most laserlike focus, the programmer will put some bugs in the code. So rather than saying to the programmer, "Every time you do A, do not forget to do B," formulate some rules that will allow most bugs to be caught by the compiler and the runtime code before they have a chance to reach the user running the application, as illustrated in Figure P-2.

When we write C++ code, we should pursue three goals:

1. The program should perform the task for which it was written; for example, calculating monthly bank statements, playing music, or editing videos.
2. The program should be human-readable; that is, the source code should be written not only for a compiler but also for a human being.
3. The program should be self-diagnosing; that is, look for the bugs it contains.

These three goals are listed in decreasing order of how often they are pursued in the real programming world. The first goal is obvious to everybody; the second, to some people, and the third is the subject of this book: instead of hunting for bugs yourself, have a compiler and your executable code do it for you. They can do the dirty work, and you can free up your brain energy so you can think about the algorithms, the design —in short, the fun part.

Audience

If you have never programmed in C++, this book is not for you. It is not intended as a C++ primer. This book assumes that you are already familiar with C++ syntax and have no trouble understanding such concepts as the constructor, copy-constructor, assignment operator, destructor, operator overloading, virtual functions, exceptions, etc. It is intended for a C++ programmer with a level of proficiency ranging from near beginner to intermediate.

How This Book Is Organized

In Part I, we discuss the following three questions: in Chapter 1, we will examine the title question. Hint: it's all in the family.

In Chapter 2, we will discuss why it is better to catch bugs at compile time, if at all possible. The rest of this chapter describes how to do this.

In Chapter 3, we discuss what to do when a bug is discovered at run-time. And here we demonstrate that in order to catch errors, we will do everything we can to make writing sanity checks (i.e., a piece of code written for specific purpose of diagnosing errors) easy. Actually, the work is already done for you: Appendix A contains the code of the macros which do writing a sanity check a snap, while delivering maximum information about what happened, where, and why, without requiring much work from a programmer. In Part II we go through different types of errors, one at a time, and formulate rules that would make each of these errors (a.k.a. bugs) either impossible, or at least easy to catch. In Part III we apply all the rules and code of the Safe C++ library introduced in Part II and discuss the testing strategy that shows how to catch bugs in the most efficient manner.

We also discuss how to make your program "debuggable." One of the goals when writing a program is to make it easy to debug, and we will show how our proposed use of error handling adds to our two friends—compiler and run-time code—the third one: a debugger, especially when it is working with the code written to be debugger-friendly.

And now we are ready to go hunting for actual bugs. In Part II, we go through some of the most common types of errors in C++ code one by one, and formulate a strategy for each, or simply a rule which makes this type of error either impossible or easily caught at run-time. Then we discuss the pros and cons of each particular rule, its pluses and minuses, and its limitations. I conclude each of these chapters with the short formulation of the rule, so that if you just want to skip the discussion and get to the bottom line, you know where to look. Chapter 17 summarizes all rules in one short place, and the Appendices contain all necessary C++ files used in the book.

At this point you might be asking yourself, "So instead of saying, 'When you do A, don't forget to do B' we're instead saying, 'When you do A, follow the rule C'? How is this better? And are there more certain ways to get rid of these bugs?" Good questions. First of all, some of the problems, such as memory deallocation, could be solved on the level of language. And actually, this one is already done. It is called Java or C#. But for the purposes of this book, we assume that for some reason ranging from abundant legacy code to very strict performance requirements to an unnatural affection for our programming language, we're going to stick with C++.

Given that, the answer to the question of why following these rules is better than the old "don't forget" remonstrance is that in many cases the actual formulation of the rule is more like this:

- The original: *"When you allocate memory here, do not forget to check all the other 20 places where you need to deallocate it and also make sure that if you add another return statement to this function, you don't forget to add a cleanup there too."*
- The new formulation: *"When you allocate memory, immediately assign it to a smart pointer right here right now, then relax and forget about it."*

I think we can agree that the second way is simpler and more reliable. It's still not an iron-clad 100% guarantee that the programmer won't forget to assign the memory to a smart pointer, but it's easier to achieve and significantly more fool-proof than the original version.

It should be noted that this book does not cover multithreading. To be precise, multithreading is briefly mentioned in the discussion of memory leaks, but that's it. Multithreading is very complex and gives the programmer many opportunities to make very subtle, non-reproducible and difficult-to-find mistakes, but this is the subject of a much larger book.

I of course do not claim that the rules proposed in this book are the only correct ones. On the contrary, many programmers will passionately argue for some alternative practice, that may well be the right one for them. There are many ways to write good C++ code. But what I am claiming is the following:

- If you follow the rules described in this book in letter and in spirit (you can even add your own rules), you will develop your code faster.

- During the first minutes or hours of testing, you will catch most if not all of the errors you've put in there; therefore, you can be much less stressed while writing it.

- Finally, when you are done testing, you will be reasonably sure that your program does not contain bugs of a certain type. That's because you've added all these sanity checks and they've all passed!

And what about efficiency of the executable code? You might be concerned that all that looking for bugs won't come for free. Not to worry—in Part III, *The Joy of Bug Hunting: From Testing to Debugging to Production*, we'll discuss how to make sure the production code will be as efficient as it can be.

Conventions Used in This Book

The following typographical conventions are used in this book:

Italic
 Indicates new terms, URLs, email addresses, filenames, and file extensions.

`Constant width`
 Used for program listings, as well as within paragraphs to refer to program elements such as variable or function names, databases, data types, environment variables, statements, and keywords.

`Constant width bold`
 Shows output produced by a program.

This icon signifies a tip, suggestion, or general note.

This icon indicates a warning or caution.

Naming Conventions

I believe strongly in the importance of a naming convention. You can use any convention you like, but here is what I've chosen for this book:

- Class names are `MultipleWordsWithFirstLettersCapitalizedAndGluedTogether`; for example:

    ```
    class MyClass {
    ```

- Function names (a.k.a. methods) in those classes `FollowTheSameConvention`; example:

    ```
    MyClass(const MyClass& that);
    void DoSomething() const;
    ```

    This is because in C++ the constructor must have the same name (and the destructor a similar name) as a class, and since they are function names in the class, we might as well make all functions look the same.

- Variables have names that are `lowercase_and_glued_together_using_underscore`.

- Data members in the class follow the same convention as variables, except they have an additional underscore at the end:

    ```
    class MyClass {
    public:
      // some code

    private:
      int int_data_;
    };
    ```

The only exception to these rules is when we work with STL (i.e., Standard Template Library) classes such as `std::vector`. In this case, we use the naming conventions of the STL in order to minimize changes to your code if you decide to replace `std::vector` with `scpp::vector` (all classes defined in this book are in the namespace `scpp`). Classes such as `scpp::array` and `scpp::matrix` follow the same convention as `scpp::vector` just because they are containers similar to a vector.

One final remark before we start: all examples of the code in this book were compiled and tested on a Mac running Max OS X 10.6.8 (Snow Leopard) using the g++ compiler or XCode. I attempted to avoid anything platform-specific; however, your mileage may vary. I also made my best effort to ensure that the code of SafeC++ library provided in the Appendices is correct, and to the best of my knowledge it does not contain any bugs. Still, you use it at your own risk. All the C++ code and header files we discuss are available both at the end of this book in the Appendices, and on the website *https://github.com/vladimir-kushnir/SafeCPlusPlus*.

We have here outlined a road map. At the end of the road is better code with fewer bugs combined with higher programmer productivity and less headache, a shorter development cycle, and more proof that the code actually works correctly. Sounds good? Let's jump in.

Using Code Examples

This book is here to help you get your job done. In general, you may use the code in this book in your programs and documentation. You do not need to contact us for permission unless you're reproducing a significant portion of the code. For example, writing a program that uses several chunks of code from this book does not require permission. Selling or distributing a CD-ROM of examples from O'Reilly books does require permission. Answering a question by citing this book and quoting example code does not require permission. Incorporating a significant amount of example code from this book into your product's documentation does require permission.

We appreciate, but do not require, attribution. An attribution usually includes the title, author, publisher, and ISBN. For example: "*Safe C++* by Vladimir Kushnir. Copyright 2012 Vladimir Kushnir, 978-1-449-32093-5."

If you feel your use of code examples falls outside fair use or the permission given above, feel free to contact us at *permissions@oreilly.com*.

Safari® Books Online

 Safari Books Online (*www.safaribooksonline.com*) is an on-demand digital library that delivers expert content in both book and video form from the world's leading authors in technology and business.

Technology professionals, software developers, web designers, and business and creative professionals use Safari Books Online as their primary resource for research, problem solving, learning, and certification training.

Safari Books Online offers a range of product mixes and pricing programs for organizations, government agencies, and individuals. Subscribers have access to thousands of books, training videos, and prepublication manuscripts in one fully searchable database from publishers like O'Reilly Media, Prentice Hall Professional, Addison-Wesley Professional, Microsoft Press, Sams, Que, Peachpit Press, Focal Press, Cisco Press, John Wiley & Sons, Syngress, Morgan Kaufmann, IBM Redbooks, Packt, Adobe Press, FT Press, Apress, Manning, New Riders, McGraw-Hill, Jones & Bartlett, Course Technology, and dozens more. For more information about Safari Books Online, please visit us online.

How to Contact Us

Please address comments and questions concerning this book to the publisher:

O'Reilly Media, Inc.
1005 Gravenstein Highway North
Sebastopol, CA 95472
800-998-9938 (in the United States or Canada)

707-829-0515 (international or local)
707-829-0104 (fax)

We have a web page for this book, where we list errata, examples, and any additional information. You can access this page at:

http://oreil.ly/SafeCPP

To comment or ask technical questions about this book, send email to:

bookquestions@oreilly.com

For more information about our books, courses, conferences, and news, see our website at *http://www.oreilly.com*.

Find us on Facebook: *http://facebook.com/oreilly*

Follow us on Twitter: *http://twitter.com/oreillymedia*

Watch us on YouTube: *http://www.youtube.com/oreillymedia*

Acknowledgments

First, I would like to thank Mike Hendrickson of O'Reilly for recognizing the value of this book and encouraging me to write it.

I am very grateful to my editor, Andy Oram, who received the thorny task of editing a book written by a first-time author for whom English is a second language. Andy's editing made this book much more readable. I also appreciate his friendly way of working with an author and enjoyed our collaboration very much. I especially would like to thank Emily Quill for significantly improving the style and clarity of the text. All errors are mine.

I would like to use this opportunity to thank Dr. Valery Fradkov, who taught me programming some time ago and provided many ideas for our first programs.

I would like to thank my son Misha for his help in figuring out what the latest version of Microsoft Visual Studio is up to. And finally, I am forever grateful to my wife Daria for her support during this project.

PART I

A Bug-Hunting Strategy for C++

This part of the book offers a classification of the kinds of errors that tend to creep into C++ programs. I show the value of catching errors during compilation instead of testing, and offer basic principles to keep in mind when pursuing the specific techniques to prevent or catch bugs discussed in later chapters.

CHAPTER 1

Where Do C++ Bugs Come From?

The C++ language is unique. While practically all programming languages borrow ideas, syntax elements, and keywords from previously existing languages, C++ incorporates an entire other language—the programming language C. In fact, the creator of C++, Bjarne Stroustrup, originally called his new language "C with classes." This means that if you already had some C code used for whatever purpose, from scientific research to trading, and contemplated switching to an object-oriented language, you'd need not to do any work of porting the code: you'd just install the new C++ compiler, and it would compile your old C code and everything would work the same way. You might even think that you'd completed a transition to C++. While this last thought would be far from the truth—the code written in real C++ looks very different from the C code —this still gives an option of a gradual transition. That is, you could start with existing C code that still compiles and runs, and gradually introduce some pieces of new code written in C++, mixing them as much as you want and eventually switching to pure C ++. So the layered design of C++ was an ingenious marketing move.

However, it also had some implications: while the whole syntax of C was grandfathered into the new language, so was the philosophy and the problems. The C programming language was created by Dennis Ritchie at Bell Labs around 1969-1973 for the purpose of writing the Unix operating system. The goal was to combine the power of a high-level programming language (as opposed to writing each computer instruction in an assembler) with efficiency: that is, the produced compiled code should be as fast as possible. One of the declared principles of the new C language was that the user should not pay any penalty for the features he does not use. So, in pursuit of efficient compiled code, C did not do anything it was not explicitly asked to do by the programmer. It was built for speed, not for comfort. And this created several problems.

First, a programmer could create an array of some length and then access an element using an index outside the bounds of the array. Even more prone to abuse was that C used pointer arithmetic, where one could calculate any value whatsoever, use it as a memory address, and access that piece of memory no matter whether it was created by the program for this purpose or not. (Actually, these two problems are one and the same—just using different syntax).

A programmer could also allocate memory at runtime using the `calloc()` or `malloc()` functions and was responsible for deallocating it using the `free()` function. However, if he forgot to deallocate it or accidentally did it more than once, the results could be catastrophic.

We will go though each of these problems in more detail in Part II. The important thing to note is that while C++ inherited the whole of C with its philosophy of efficiency, it inherited all its problems as well. So part of the answer to the question of where the bugs come from is "from C."

However, this is not the end of the story. In addition to the problems inherited from C, C++ introduced a few of its own. For instance, most people count friend functions and multiple inheritance as bad ideas. And C++ has its own method of allocating memory: instead of calling functions like `calloc()` or `malloc()`, one should use the operator `new`. The `new` operator does more then just allocating memory; it creates objects, i.e., calls their constructors. And in the same spirit as C, the deallocation of this memory using the `delete` operator is the responsibility of the programmer. So far the situation seems to be analogous to the one in C: you allocate memory, and then you delete it. However, the complication is that there are two different `new` operators in C++:

```
MyClass* p_object = new MyClass();  // Create one object
MyClass* p_array = new MyClass[number_of_elements]; // Create an array
```

In the first case, `new` creates one object of type `MyClass`, and in the second, it creates an array of objects of the same type. Correspondingly, there are two different `delete` operators:

```
delete p_object;
delete [] p_array;
```

And of course, once you've used "new with brackets" to create objects, you need to use "delete with brackets" to delete them. So a new type of mistake is possible: the cross-use of new and delete, one with brackets and another without. If you mess up here, you can wreak havoc on the memory heap. So to summarize, the bugs in C++ mostly came from C, but C++ added this new method for programmers to shoot themselves in the foot, and we'll discuss it in Part II.

CHAPTER 2

When to Catch a Bug

Why the Compiler Is Your Best Place to Catch Bugs

Given the choice of catching bugs at compile time vs. catching bugs at runtime, the short answer is that you want to catch bugs at compile time if at all possible. There are multiple reasons for this. First, if a bug is detected by the compiler, you will receive a message in plain English saying exactly where, in which file and at which line, the error has occurred. (I may be slightly optimistic here, because in some cases—especially when STL is involved—compilers produce error messages so cryptic that it takes an effort to figure out what exactly the compiler is unhappy about. But compilers are getting better all the time, and most of the time they are pretty clear about what the problem is.)

Another reason is that a complete compilation (with a final link) covers all the code in the program, and if the compiler returns with no errors or warnings, you can be 100% sure that there are no errors that could be detected at compile time in your program. You could never say the same thing about run-time testing; with a large enough piece of code, it is difficult to guarantee that all the possible branches were tested, that every line of code was executed at least once.

And even if you could guarantee that, it wouldn't be enough—the same piece of code could work correctly with one set of inputs and incorrectly with another, so with run-time testing you are never completely sure that you have tested everything.

And finally, there is the time factor: you compile before you run your code, so if you catch your error during compilation, you've saved some time. Some runtime errors appear late in the program, so it might take minutes or even hours of running to get to an error. Moreover, the error might not be even reproducible—it could appear and disappear at consecutive runs in a seemingly random manner. Compared to all that, catching errors at compile time seems like child's play!

How to Catch Bugs in the Compiler

By now you should be convinced that whenever possible, it's best to catch errors at compile time. But how can we achieve this? Let's look at a couple of examples.

The first is the story of a `Variant` class. Once upon a time, a software company was writing an Excel plug-in. This is a file that, after being opened by Microsoft Excel, adds some new functions that could be called from an Excel cell. Because the Excel cell can contain data of different types—an integer (e.g., 1), a floating-point number (e.g., 3.1415926535), a calendar date (such as 1/1/2000), or even a string ("This is the house that Jack built")—the company developed a `Variant` class that behaved like a chameleon and could contain any of these data types. But then someone had the idea that a `Variant` could contain another `Variant`, and even a vector of `Variant`s (i.e., `std::vector<Variant>`). And these `Variant`s started being used not just to communicate with Excel, but also in internal code. So when looking at the function signature:

```
Variant SomeFunction(const Variant& input);
```

it became totally impossible to understand what kind of data the function expects on input and what kind of data it returns. So if for example it expects a calendar date and you pass it a string that does not resemble a date, this can be detected only at runtime. As we've just discussed, finding errors at compile time is preferable, so this approach prevents us from using the compiler to catch bugs early using type safety. The solution to this problem will be discussed below, but the short answer is that you should use separate C++ classes to represent different data types.

The preceding example is real but somewhat extreme. Here is a more typical situation. Suppose we are processing some financial data, such as the price of a stock, and we accompany each value with the correspondent time stamp, i.e., the date and time when this price was observed. So how do we measure time? The simplest solution is to count seconds since some time in the past (say, since 1/1/1970).

Suddenly someone realizes that the library used for this purpose provides a 32-bit integer, which has a maximum value of about 2 billion, after which the value will overflow and become negative. This would happen about 68 years after the starting point on the time axis, i.e., in the year 2038. The resulting problem is analogous to the famous "Y2K" problem, and fixing it would entail going through a rather large number of files and finding all these variables and making them `int64`, which has 64 bits instead of 32, and this would last about 4 billion times longer, which should be enough even for the most outrageous optimist.

But by now another problem has turned up: some programmers used `int64 num_of_seconds`, while others used `int64_num_of_millisec`, while still others wrote `int64 num_of_microsec`. The compiler has absolutely no way of figuring out if a function that expects time in milliseconds is being passed time in microseconds or vice versa. Of course, if we make some assumptions that the time interval in which we want to analyze our stock prices starts after, say, year 1990 and goes until some point in the future, say year 3000, then we can add a sanity check at runtime that the value being passed must fall into this interval. However, multiple functions need to be equipped with this sanity check, which requires a lot of human work. And what if someone later decides to go back and analyze the stock prices throughout the 20th century?

The Proper Way to Handle Types

Now, this entire mess could have been easily avoided altogether if we had just created a Time class and left the details of when it starts and what unit it measures (seconds, milliseconds, etc.) as hidden details of the internal implementation. One advantage of this approach is that if we mistakenly try to pass some other data type instead of time (which now has a Time type), a compiler would have caught it early. Another advantage is that if the Time class is currently implemented using milliseconds and we later decide to increase the accuracy to microseconds, we need only edit one class, where we can change this detail of internal implementation without affecting the rest of the code.

So how do we catch these types of errors at compile time instead of runtime? We can start by having a separate class for each type of data. Let's use int for integers, double for floating-point data, std::string for text, Date for calendar dates, Time for time, and so on for all the other types of data. But simply doing this is not enough. Suppose we have two classes, Apple and Orange, and a function that expects an input of a type Orange:

```
void DoSomethingWithOrange(const Orange& orange);
```

However, we accidentally could provide an object of type Apple instead:

```
Apple an_apple(some_inputs);
DoSomethingWithOrange(an_apple);
```

This might compile under some circumstances, because the C++ compiler is trying to do us a favor and will silently convert Apple to Orange if it can. This can happen in two ways:

1. If the Orange class has a constructor taking only one argument of type Apple
2. If the Apple class has an operator that converts it to Orange

The first case happens when the class Orange looks like this:

```
class Orange {
 public:
   Orange(const Apple& apple);
   // more code
};
```

It can even look like this:

```
class Orange {
 public:
   Orange(const Apple& apple, const Banana* p_banana=0);
   // more code
};
```

Even though in the last example the constructor looks like it has two inputs, it can be called with only one argument, so it can also serve to implicitly convert `Apple` into `Orange`. The solution to this problem is to declare these constructors with keyword `explicit`. This prevents the compiler from doing an automatic (implicit) conversion, so we force the programmer to use `Orange` where `Orange` is expected:

```
class Orange {
 public:
  explicit Orange(const Apple& apple);
  // more code
};
```

and correspondingly in the second case:

```
class Orange {
 public:
  explicit Orange(const Apple& apple, const Banana* p_banana=0);
  // more code
};
```

Another method that lets the compiler know how to convert an `Apple` into an `Orange` is to provide a conversion operator:

```
class Apple {
 public:
  // constructors and other code …
  operator Orange () const;
};
```

The very presence of this operator suggests that the programmer made an explicit effort to provide the compiler with a way to convert `Apple` into `Orange`, and therefore it might not be a mistake. However, the absence of the keyword `explicit` in front of the constructor could easily be a mistake, so it's advisable to declare all constructors that could be called with one argument with keyword `explicit`. In general, any possibility of implicit conversions is a bad idea, so if you want to provide a way of converting `Apple` into `Orange` inside the class `Apple`, as in the previous example, the better way of doing so is:

```
class Apple {
 public:
  // constructors and other code …
  Orange AsOrange() const;
};
```

In this case, in order to convert an `Apple` into an `Orange` you would need to write:

```
Apple apple(some_inputs);
DoSomethingWithOrange(apple.AsOrange()); // explicit conversion
```

There is one more way to mix up different data types: by using enum. Consider the following example: suppose we defined the following two enums for days of the week and for months:

```
enum { SUN, MON, TUE, WED, THU, FRI, SAT };
enum { JAN=1, FEB, MAR, APR, MAY, JUN, JUL, AUG, SEP, OCT, NOV, DEC };
```

All of these constants are actually integers (e.g., C built-in type int), and if we have a function that expects as an input a day of the week:

```
void FunctionExpectingDayOfWeek(int day_of_week);
```

the following call will compile without any warnings:

```
FunctionExpectingDayOfWeek(JAN);
```

And there is not much we can do at run time because both JAN and MON are integers equal to 1. The way to catch this bug is not to use "plain vanilla" enums that create integers, but to use enums to create new types:

```
typedef enum { SUN, MON, TUE, WED, THU, FRI, SAT } DayOfWeek;
typedef enum { JAN=1, FEB, MAR, APR, MAY, JUN, JUL, AUG, SEP, OCT, NOV, DEC } Month;
```

In this case, the function expecting a day of week should be declared like this:

```
void FunctionExpectingDayOfWeek(DayOfWeek day_of_week);
```

An attempt to call it with a Month like this:

```
FunctionExpectingDayOfWeek(JAN);
```

results in a compilation error:

```
error: cannot convert 'Month' to 'DayOfWeek' for
        argument '1' to 'void
        FunctionExpectingDayOfWeek(DayOfWeek)'
```

which is exactly what we would want in this case.

This approach has a downside, however. In the case when enum creates integer constants, you can write a code like this:

```
for(int month=JAN; month<=DEC; ++month)
  cout << "Month = " << month << endl;
```

But when the enum is used to create a new *type*, the following:

```
for(Month month=JAN; month<=DEC; ++month)
  cout << "Month = " << month << endl;
```

does not compile. So if you need to iterate through the values of your enum, you are stuck with integers.

Of course, there are exceptions to any rule, and sometimes programmers will have reasons to write classes such as Variant for the specific purpose of allowing implicit conversions. However, most of the time it is a good idea to avoid implicit conversions altogether: this allows you to use the full power of the compiler to check types of different variables to catch our potential errors early—at compile time.

Now suppose that we've done everything we can to use type safety to the fullest extent possible. Unfortunately, with the exceptions of types bool and char, the number of different values that each type can contain is astronomically high, and usually only a small portion of these values makes sense. For instance, if we use the type double for the price of a stock, we can be reasonably sure that the value will be between 0 and

10,000 (with the sole exception of the stock of the Berkshire Hathaway company, whose owner Warren Buffet apparently does not believe that it is a good idea to keep the stock price within a reasonable range and has therefore never split the stock, which at the time of this writing is above $100,000 per share). Still, even Berkshire Hathaway uses only a small portion of the range of a double precision number, which can be as large as 10^{308} and can also be negative, which does not make sense for a stock price. Since for most types only a small portion of all possible values makes sense, there will always be errors that can be diagnosed only at runtime.

In fact, most of the problems of the C language, such as specifying an index out of bounds or accessing memory improperly through pointer arithmetic, can be diagnosed only at runtime. For this reason, the rest of this book is dedicated mainly to the discussion of catching runtime errors.

Rules for this chapter for diagnosing errors at compile time:

- Prohibit implicit type conversions: declare constructors taking one parameter with the keyword `explicit` and avoid conversion operators.
- Use different classes for different data types.
- Do not use `enums` to create `int` constants; use them to create new types.

CHAPTER 3

What to Do When We Encounter an Error at Runtime

There are two types of runtime errors: those that are the result of programmer error (that is, *bugs*) and those that would happen even if the code were absolutely correct. An example of the second type occurs when a user mistypes a username or password. Other examples occur when the program needs to open a file, but the file is missing or the program doesn't have permission to open it, or the program tries to access the Internet but the connection doesn't work. In short, even if the program is perfect, things such as wrong inputs and hardware issues can produce problems.

In this book we concentrate on catching run-time errors of the first type, a.k.a. bugs. A piece of code written for the specific purpose of catching bugs will be called a *sanity check*. When a sanity check fails, i.e., a bug is discovered, this should do two things:

1. Provide as much information as possible about the error, i.e., where it has occurred and why, including all values of the relevant variables.

2. Take an appropriate action.

What is an appropriate action? We'll discuss this later in more detail, but the shortest answer is to terminate the program. First, let's concentrate on the information about the bug, called the error message. To diagnose a bug we provide a macro defined in the *scpp_assert.hpp* file:

```
#define SCPP_ASSERT(condition, msg)        \
  if(!(condition)) {                       \
    std::ostringstream s;                  \
    s << msg;                              \
    SCPP_AssertErrorHandler(               \
      __FILE__, __LINE__, s.str().c_str());\
  }
```

SCPP_AssertErrorHandler is the function declared in the same file. (As it was mentioned earlier, the code of all C++ files cited in this book is available both in the Appendices and online at *https://github.com/vladimir-kushnir/SafeCPlusPlus*.)

First, let's see how it works. Suppose you have the following code in the *my_test.cpp* file:

```cpp
#include <iostream>
#include "scpp_assert.hpp"

using namespace std;

int main(int argc, char* argv[]) {
  cout << "Hello, SCPP_ASSERT" << endl;

  double stock_price = 100.0;   // Reasonable price
  SCPP_ASSERT(0. < stock_price && stock_price <= 1.e6,
    "Stock price " << stock_price << " is out of range");

  stock_price = -1.0; // Not a reasonable value
  SCPP_ASSERT(0. < stock_price && stock_price <= 1.e6,
    "Stock price " << stock_price << " is out of range");

  return 0;
}
```

Compiling and running the example will produce the following output:

```
Hello, SCPP_ASSERT Stock price -1 is out of range in file
      my_test.cpp #16
```

The macro automatically provides the filename and line number where the error occurred. What's going on in here? The macro SCPP_ASSERT takes two parameters: a condition and an error message. If the condition is true, nothing happens, and the code execution continues. If the condition is false, the message gets streamed into an ostringstream object, and the function SCPP_AssertErrorHandler() is called. Why do we need to stream the message into the ostringstream object? Why can't we just pass the message to the error handler function directly?

The reason is that this intermediate step allows us not just to use simple error messages like this:

```cpp
SCPP_ASSERT(index < array.size(), "Index is out of bounds.");
```

but to *compose* a meaningful error message that contains much more information about an error:

```cpp
SCPP_ASSERT(index < array.size(),
  "Index " << index << " is out of bounds " << array.size());
```

In this macro you can use any objects of any class that has a << operator. Suppose you have a class:

```cpp
class MyClass {
 public:
  // Returns true if the object is in OK state.
  bool IsValid() const;

  // Allow this function access to the private data of this class
  friend std::ostream& operator <<(std::ostream& os, const MyClass& obj);
};
```

All you need to do is provide an operator << as follows:

```
inline std::ostream& operator <<(std::ostream& os, const MyClass& obj) {
  // Do something in here to show the state of the object in
  // a human-readable form.
  return os;
}
```

and you can use an object of the type MyClass to compose a message:

```
MyClass obj(some_inputs);
SCPP_ASSERT(obj.IsValid(), "Object " << obj << " is invalid.");
```

Thus, if you run your program and the sanity check detects an error, chances are that you won't need to repeat the process in the debugger to figure out what exactly happened and why. But doing this sanity check might slow down your program, and the reason we're using C++ is we want our code to run as fast as possible. And indeed, sanity checks do slow down the code, some of them significantly (as we'll see later when dealing with the Index Out Of Bounds error in Chapter 4). To deal with this problem, some of the sanity checks are made temporary—for testing only. For this purpose, the *scpp_assert.hpp* file defines a second macro, SCPP_TEST_ASSERT:

```
#ifdef SCPP_TEST_ASSERT_ON
#define SCPP_TEST_ASSERT(condition,msg) SCPP_ASSERT(condition, msg)
#else
#define SCPP_TEST_ASSERT(condition,msg) // do nothing
#endif
```

The difference between this SCPP_TEST_ASSERT and the previous SCPP_ASSERT is that SCPP_ASSERT is a permanent sanity check, whereas SCPP_TEST_ASSERT can be switched on and off during compilation (more about this in Chapter 15). Now let's return to the second question of what to do when a bug is discovered at runtime: what is the appropriate action in this case? Actually, there are only two choices:

1. Terminate the program.
2. Throw an exception.

The code of the error handler function provided in the *scpp_assert.cpp* file gives you both opportunities:

```
void SCPP_AssertErrorHandler(const char* file_name,
                             unsigned line_number,
                             const char* message) {
  // This is a good place to put your debug breakpoint:
  // You can also add writing of the same info into a log file
  // if appropriate.

#ifdef SCPP_THROW_EXCEPTION_ON_BUG
  throw scpp::ScppAssertFailedException(
    file_name, line_number, message);
#else
  cerr << message << " in file " << file_name
       << " #" << line_number << endl << flush;
  // Terminate application
```

```
    exit(1);
#endif
}
```

As you can see from the code of the error handler, it could do either of the two possible actions, depending on whether the symbol `SCPP_THROW_EXCEPTION_ON_BUG` is defined. In the most common case, when you want to test your code until you find the first bug, the simplest action by default is to terminate the program, fix the bug, and start over, which is achieved when the symbol `SCPP_THROW_EXCEPTION_ON_BUG` is not defined. In this case the error handler will print the message and terminate the application.

There are some situations when at least some of the sanity checks are left active in the code even in production mode. Suppose you have a program that does continuous sequential processing of a large number of requests, one after another, and while processing one of the requests it ran into a bug, i.e., the sanity check failed. It might so happen that the program could continue to process some of (and maybe even most of) the other requests. In some situations it might be important to continue to process these requests as much as possible—because it'll keep clients happy, because there's a serious amount of money involved, etc. In such cases, terminating the program on a failure of a sanity check is not an option. The way to proceed in these situations is to throw an exception containing a description of what happened from the error handler, catch it somewhere in the top level of the code, document it in some log file, maybe send some email or pager alerts, declare the current attempt to process the request a failure, and at the same time continue with all the others.

To illustrate this, an exception class that is declared in the same *scpp_assert.hpp* file:

```
namespace scpp {
class ScppAssertFailedException : public std::exception {
 public:
   ScppAssertFailedException(const char* file_name,
                             unsigned line_number,
                             const char* message);

   virtual const char* what() const throw () {
     return what_.c_str();
   }

   virtual ~ScppAssertFailedException() throw () {}

 private:
   std::string what_;
};
} // namespace scpp
```

If you are strict about exception types, you can pass to the error handler an enum containing information about error type, and throw different types of exceptions for different types of errors. But this book demonstrates a general approach to writing code with the explicit goal of self-diagnosing bugs, so we'll stick with the simplest possible case of one exception class. In this case, the code example that would trigger the sanity check would look like this:

```cpp
#include <iostream>
#include "scpp_assert.hpp"

using namespace std;

int main(int argc, char* argv[]) {
  cout << "Hello, SCPP_ASSERT" << endl;

  try {
    double stock_price = 100.0;   // Reasonable price
    SCPP_ASSERT(0 < stock_price && stock_price <= 1e6,
      "Stock price " << stock_price << " is out of range.");

    stock_price = -1.; // Not a reasonable value
    SCPP_ASSERT(0 < stock_price && stock_price <= 1e6,
      "Stock price " << stock_price << " is out of range.");

  } catch (const exception& ex) {
    cerr << "Exception caught in " << __FILE__ << " #" << __LINE__ << ":\n"
        << ex.what() << endl;
  }

  return 0;
}
```

Running this example leads to the following output:

```
Hello, SCPP_ASSERT Exception caught in
    scpp_assert_exception_test.cpp #20: SCPP assertion failed with message
    'Stock price -1 is out of range.' in file scpp_assert_exception_test.cpp
    #17.
```

Note that here we also receive additional information—not only where the error has occurred but also where it was caught, which could be a useful hint when trying to figure out what exactly happened before involving a debugger.

Another question is why we need to call a SCPP_AssertErrorHandler function located in a separate *scpp_assert.cpp* file instead of doing the same thing inside the macro in the *scpp_assert.hpp* file. The short answer is that debuggers usually prefer to step through the functions as opposted to stepping through macros. We'll return to this subject in Chapter 15.

Now we have two macros: one to use in production and one for testing only. When should you use each one? As the author of your program, only you can answer this question. Typically, you should have a feeling for how often the function that will contain a sanity check called, how long it takes to execute, and how long the evaluation of the sanity check will take as compared to the execution of the function itself.

If you know that the function is called rarely or maybe even just once for initialization purposes, and the sanity checks are cheap, then go ahead and use the permanent macro.

You might be glad you did when a problem is reported from the field. In other cases, use the temporary macro.

Note that when evaluating how long the sanity check takes, all that matters is how long it takes to evaluate the Boolean condition. How long it takes to compose a message is not relevant: if you get to that stage, you are in no rush at all.

Different sanity checks slow down your program to different extents. One of the worst in this regard, the index-out-of-bounds sanity check, will be discussed in Chapter 4. So you might add some more granularity to this process and define different macros for different types of bugs, if some of them are slowing testing too much. Feel free to experiment with what works best for your code.

We now have macros that allow us to write sanity checks easily and still compose a meaningful error message. When do we write them? If you think: "I will write my code and then return and add sanity checks," chances are it will never happen. Also, while you are writing your code, the picture of what is going on in it and which conditions should be true or false is in the freshest possible state in your brain. So the answer is to write sanity checks *while* you are writing the code. Any time you can think of any condition you can check for—write a sanity check for it. Even better, when you start writing a new function, start with writing sanity checks for all inputs *before* you write anything else.

"But this is a lot of additional work!" you might think. True, but as we've seen, writing sanity checks is not difficult, and more importantly it will pay off later at the testing stage. It is much easier to write sanity checks while you have a mental picture of the algorithm in your head than have to go back and debug the code later.

In Part II, we'll consider some of the most common mistakes in C++ code and learn how to deal with them—one at a time.

Bug Hunting: One Bug at a Time

This section gives detailed advice, along with directions for using the Safe C++ library I created, for catching particular bugs before your code goes out in production.

CHAPTER 4

Index Out of Bounds

There are several ways in C++ to create an array of objects of some type T. Three common methods are:

```
#define N 10  // array size N is known at compile time
  T static_array[N];

  int n = 20; // array size n is calculated at runtime
  T* dynamic_array = new T[n];

  std::vector<T> vector_array; // array size can be changed at runtime
```

Of course, you can still use the `calloc()` and `malloc()` functions and your program will compile and run, but it's not a good idea to mix C and C++ unless you have to because you're relying on legacy C libraries. However you allocate the array, you can access an element in it using an unsigned integer index:

```
const T& element_of_static_array  = static_array[index];
const T& element_of_dynamic_array = dynamic_array[index];
const T& element_of_vector_array  = vector_array[index];
```

Let's deal with dynamic arrays and vectors first, and return to the static array later in this chapter.

Dynamic Arrays

What would happen if we provide an `index` value that is larger than or equal to the array size? In all three of the preceding examples, the code will silently return garbage. (The exception to this rule for Microsoft Visual Studio 2010 is discussed later.) The situation is even worse if you decide to use the operator [] in the left-hand side of an assignment:

```
some_array[index] = x;
```

Depending on your luck (or lack of thereof) you might overwrite some other unrelated variable, an element of another array, or even a program instruction, and in the latter case your program will most likely crash. Each of these errors also provides opportunities for malicious intruders to take over your program and turn it to bad ends. However, the std::vector provides an at(index) function, which does bounds checking by throwing an out_of_range exception. The problem with this is that if you want to do this sanity check, you have to rigorously use the at() function everywhere for accessing an array element. And naturally, this slows your code down, so once you are done testing, you'll want to replace it everywhere with the [] operator, which is faster. But doing that replacement requires massive editing of your code, which is a lot of work, followed by a need to retest it, because during that tedious process you could accidentally mistype something.

So instead of the at() function, I suggest the following. Although a dynamic array leaves the [] operator totally out of your control, the STL vector implements it as a C++ function that we can rewrite according to our bug-hunting goals. And that's what we'll do here. In the file *scpp_vector.hpp* we redefine the [] operators as follows:

```
T& operator [] (size_type index) {
  SCPP_TEST_ASSERT(index < std::vector<T>::size(),
    "Index " << index << " must be less than "
            << std::vector<T>::size());
  return std::vector<T>:: operator[](index);
}

const T& operator [] (size_type index) const {
  SCPP_TEST_ASSERT(index < std::vector<T>::size(),
    "Index " << index << " must be less than "
            << std::vector<T>::size());
  return std::vector<T>::operator[](index);
}
```

Let's see how this works. Here is an example of how to use it (including—intentionally —how *not* to use it):

```
#include <iostream>
#include "scpp_vector.hpp"

using namespace std;

int main() {
  scpp::vector<int> vect;
  for(int i=0; i<3; ++i)
    vect.push_back(i);

  cout << "My vector = " << vect << endl;

  for(int i=0; i<=vect.size(); ++i)
    cout << "Value of vector at " << i << " is " << vect[i] << endl;

  return 0;
}
```

First, note that instead of writing `std::vector<int>` or just `vector<int>` we wrote `scpp::vector<int>`. This is to distinguish our vector from the STL's vector. By using our `scpp::vector` we replace the standard implementation—in this case, the implementation of `operator []`—by our own safe implementation, and you will see the same approach to preventing other bugs later in this book. `scpp::vector` also gives you a `<<` operator for free, so you can print your vector as long as it is not too big, and as long as the type `T` defines the `<<` operator.

The next thing to notice is that in the second loop, instead of writing `i<vect.size()` we wrote `i<=vect.size()`. This is a very common programming error, and we did it just to see what happens when the index is out of bounds. Indeed, the program produces the following output:

```
My vector = 0 1 2

   Value of vector at 0 is 0

   Value of vector at 1 is 1 Value of vector at 2 is 2

   Index 3 must be less than 3 in file scpp_vector.hpp
       #17
```

This sanity check works as long as the symbol `SCPP_TEST_ASSERT_ON` is defined, and is easy to switch on and off at compile time when necessary. The problem with this approach is that the vector's `[]` operator is very often used inside loops, so this sanity check is used a lot and therefore slows the program down significantly just as using `at()` would. If you feel that this is becoming a problem in your program, feel free to define a new macro, such as `SCPP_TEST_ASSERT_INDEX_OUT_OF_BOUNDS`, which would work exactly the same way as `SCPP_TEST_ASSERT` but would be used only inside `scpp::vector::operator[]`. `SCPP_TEST_ASSERT_INDEX_OUT_OF_BOUNDS` should differ from `SCPP_TEST_ASSERT` only by the fact that it can be switched on and off independently of the `SCPP_TEST_ASSERT` macro, so you can deactivate it after you are sure that your code does not have this bug while keeping the rest of your sanity checks active.

In addition to allowing you to catch this index-out-of-bounds error, the template vector has one advantage over statically and dynamically allocated arrays: its size grows as needed (as long as you don't run out of memory). However, this advantage comes at a cost. The vector, if not told in advance how much memory will be needed, allocates some default amount (called its "capacity"). When the actual size reaches this capacity, the vector will allocate a bigger chunk of memory, copy old data into the new memory area, and release the old chunk of memory. So from time to time, adding a new element to a template vector could suddenly become slow. Therefore, if you know in advance what number of elements you will need, as with both static and dynamically allocated arrays, tell the vector up front, for instance, in the constructor:

```
scpp::vector<int> vect(n);
```

This creates a vector with a specified number of elements in it. You could also write:

```
scpp::vector<int> vect(n, 0);
```

which would also initialize all elements to a specified value (in this case zero, but any other value will work too).

An alternative is to create a vector with zero elements in it but to specify the desired capacity:

```
scpp::vector<int> vect;
vect.reserve(n);
```

The difference between this example and the previous one is that in this case the vector is empty (i.e., `vect.size()` returns 0), but when you start adding elements to it, you will not run into the incrementing capacity procedure with the corresponding slow-down until you reach the size of *n*.

Can We Derive from std::vector?

At this point you may have looked at the definition of the `scpp::vector` in the *scpp_vector.hpp* file:

```
namespace scpp {
template <typename T>
class vector : public std::vector<T> {
```

You may have asked yourself whether it is a good idea to derive a class from a base class that does not have a virtual destructor. Indeed, if we have the following situation:

```
class Base {
  // not virtual !!!
  ~Base();
};

class Derived : public Base {
  // also not virtual !!!
  ~Derived() {
    // some non-trivial code releasing resources
  }
}
```

and we use these classes like this:

```
Base* p = new Derived;
// some code using p
delete p;
```

the `delete` statement will actually call the destructor of the base class `~Base()` and none of the code of the `~Derived()` destructor will be executed, thus leading to unreleased resources such as memory leaks, etc. The same situation will occur even if we did not write any non-trivial code in the `~Derived()` destructor, but added to the derived class some new data members that do have non-trivial destructors, such as containers or smart pointers. Even though we do not write the `~Derived()` code ourselves, the compiler will do it for us, calling all the destructors of the added data members. In the

---

example just shown, this ~Derived() destructor will not be called, which represents a problem. However, in our concrete example of scpp::vector, the situation is different:

- We do not expect these two classes to be used in the manner of std::vector* p_vect = new scpp::vector. scpp::vector must be used as a plain vector, as if it was never derived from anything.

- We did not add any data members to scpp::vector, and its destructor does not do any work except to call the destructor of the base class. Even if we did something like what is described in the previous example with Base and Derived, in this particular case nothing bad will happened.

- If this violation of C++ purity still bothers you, you could use composition instead of derivation, e.g., write a scpp::vector that *contains* std::vector as a private data member, and wrap each of its methods in the corresponding method of the derived class, which is a lot of coding but would produce the same results as my implementation.

There is one more consequence of this derivation: if you have any function that expects std::vector, you can still pass to it scpp::vector, which is being publicly derived from the former, and therefore *is* a std::vector. Here is an example:

```
void FunctionTakingRefToSTLVector(const std::vector<int>& v) {
  cout << "ATTENTION, we are about to test index-out-of-bounds "
       << "for STL vector reference to scpp::vector" << endl << flush;

  for(int i=0; i<=v.size(); ++i)
    cout << "Value of vector at " << i << " is " << v[i] << endl;
}

int main() {
  scpp::vector<int> v;
  for(int i=0; i<3; ++i)
    v.push_back(i);
  cout << "Initial vector: " << v << endl;

  FunctionTakingRefToSTLVector(v);
}
```

The vector created here has three elements, and the FunctionTakingRefToSTLVector() function tries to access an element with index 3, which is out of bounds. This code produces the following output:

```
ATTENTION, we are about to test index-out-of-bounds for
        STL vector reference to scpp::vector

        Value of vector at 0 is 0

        Value of vector at 1 is 1

        Value of vector at 2 is 2

        Value of vector at 3 is 1
```

Note that the code happily prints the value at the index 3, even though the maximum valid index is 2, which means that our sanity check did not work inside `Function TakingRefToSTLVector()`. The reason is that the function uses the original `[]` operator of `std::vector` because the version used is determined by the type of the reference to the vector, which in this case comes from the declaration in the function's argument list, `const std::vector<int>&`. The `[]` operator was never declared as *virtual*, and we couldn't do so if we wanted to because the declaration is in the code of the STL vector. Declaring it virtual would not be a good idea anyway because it would slow it down. So this is a risk of our approach. To make it work, you must be careful to use `scpp::vector` everywhere you want the sanity check to be active.

On the other hand, if you have a function taking `std::vector <T>&` and you trust that this function has already been tested, you can keep the original signature taking `std::vector <T>&` and it will run faster. At the same time, outside of this function you will be taking full advantage of checking for index-out-of bounds errors in the rest of the code.

Static Arrays

Now, as promised, let's deal with the static array:

```
#define N 10  // array size N is known at compile time
  T static_array[N];
```

Here, the size is known at compile time and will not change. Of course, to use the safe array with its boundary check, you can use a template vector with the size specified in a constructor:

```
scpp::vector vect(N);
```

This will work exactly the same as the static array, but the problem here is efficiency. While the static array allocates its memory on stack, the template vector allocates memory inside the constructor using the `new` operator, and this is a relatively slow operation. If runtime efficiency is important in your case, it's better to use a template array, defined as follows in the *scpp_array.hpp* file:

```
namespace scpp {

// Fixed-size array
template <typename T, unsigned N>
class array {
 public:
  typedef unsigned size_type;

  // Most commonly used constructors:
  array() {}

  explicit array(const T& initial_value) {
    for(size_type i=0; i<size(); ++i)
      data_[i] = initial_value;
```

```
    }

    size_type size() const { return N; }

    // Note: we do not provide a copy constructor and assignment operator.
    // We rely on the default versions of these methods generated by the compiler.

    T& operator[] (size_type index) {
      SCPP_TEST_ASSERT(index < N,
        "Index " << index << " must be less than " << N);
      return data_[index];
    }

    const T& operator [] (size_type index) const {
      SCPP_TEST_ASSERT(index < N,
        "Index " << index << " must be less than " << N);
      return data_[index];
    }

    // Accessors emulating iterators:
    T* begin() { return &data_[0]; }
    const T* begin()const { return &data_[0]; }

    // Returns an iterator PAST the end of the array.
    T* end() { return &data_[N]; }
    const T* end()const { return &data_[N]; }

  private:
    T data_[N];
};
} // namespace scpp
```

This array behaves exactly like a static C array. However, when compiled with the sanity check macro SCPP_TEST_ASSERT active, it provides an index-out-of-bounds check. The begin() and end() methods are provided to simulate iterators, so that you can use this array in some of the situations where you would have used the template vectors—for example, to sort numbers. The following code demonstrates how to sort this array using STL's sort algorithm:

```
#include <algorithm>

scpp::array<int, 5> a(0);
a[0] = 7;
a[1] = 2;
a[2] = 3;
a[3] = 9;
a[4] = 0;

cout << "Array before sort: " << a << endl;
sort(a.begin(), a.end());
cout << "Array after sort: " << a <<
endl;
```

This produces the following output:

```
Array before sort: 7 2 3 9 0

Array after sort: 0 2 3 7 9
```

As a side benefit, you also get a << operator, which allows you to stream an array as shown in the previous example, assuming it is not too large and the template type T has a << operator. Of course, the use of this fixed-sized array must be limited to cases where the array size N is not too large. Otherwise, you'll be spending your stack memory, a limited resource, on this array.

So the advice in this section is not to use static or dynamically allocated arrays, but a template vector or array instead. This solves another problem described in Chapter 1: when you use the new operator with brackets, you need to use the delete operator with brackets as well. If you cross-use these operators (new with brackets and delete without or vice versa) you will corrupt the memory heap, which generally leads to bad consequences. Once we decide not to use dynamically allocated arrays, which are created through the new operator with brackets, we've killed two birds with one stone: the problem of an index out of bounds, and the problem of mixing operators with and without brackets. In short, do not use the new operator (and the corresponding delete operator) with brackets. Your life will be easier.

 At the time of this writing, the newest version of Microsoft Visual Studio 2010 Ultimate diagnoses the index-out-of-bounds error in std:: vector when compiled in a Debug mode, and pops up a dialog box (Figure 4-1).

This dialog offers you the choice to Ignore, Abort, or Retry (in which case you can debug the application). While "Ignore" seems appropriate only if you are extremely adventurous, one can hope that the rest of the compilers working under Unix, Linux, and Mac OS will catch up to the trend.

Multidimensional Arrays

Now that we've settled on the use of a template vector or array as an implementation of a linear array, let's consider what to do if you need a two-dimensional matrix, a three-dimensional array, or generally speaking, an *n*-dimensional array. Because all the issues in the general case of *n*-dimensional arrays can be illustrated using a two-dimensional matrix, we will limit our discussion to this case and call it simply a matrix, with the understanding that the same principles apply to three or more dimensions.

If the size of the matrix is known at compile time, you can easily implement it as an array of arrays, and be done with it. Therefore, we'll concentrate on the more complex case of a matrix whose size is calculated at run time. Such a matrix can easily be created

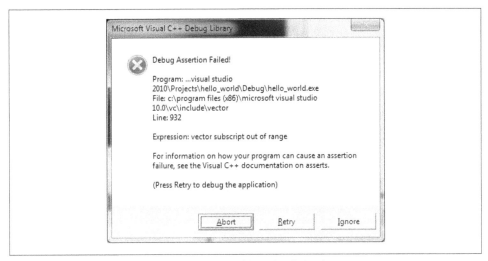

Figure 4-1. Microsoft Visual Studio "Index out of bounds" dialog box

as a vector of vectors, and in fact this approach is the only one possible if different rows must be of different lengths. However, most of the time all rows should be of the same length (e.g., the matrix is rectangular or even quadratic), and in this case the approach of using a vector of vectors is inefficient: it requires multiple memory allocations, which is a relatively slow operation (and the same can be said about deallocation). Because our goal in using C++ is efficiency, we'll try a different approach and create a rectangular matrix using only one memory allocation, as shown in the class matrix in the *scpp_matrix.hpp* file:

```
// Two-dimensional rectangular matrix.
template <typename T>
class matrix {
 public:
  typedef unsigned size_type;

  matrix(size_type num_rows, size_type num_cols)
    : rows_(num_rows), cols_(num_cols), data_(num_rows * num_cols)
  {
    SCPP_TEST_ASSERT(num_rows > 0,
      "Number of rows in a matrix must be positive");
    SCPP_TEST_ASSERT(num_cols > 0,
      "Number of columns in a matrix must be positive");
  }

  matrix(size_type num_rows, size_type num_cols, const T& init_value)
    : rows_(num_rows), cols_(num_cols), data_(num_rows * num_cols, init_value)
  {
    SCPP_TEST_ASSERT(num_rows > 0,
      "Number of rows in a matrix must be positive");
    SCPP_TEST_ASSERT(num_cols > 0,
      "Number of columns in a matrix must be positive");
  }
```

```
  size_type num_rows() const { return rows_; }
  size_type num_cols() const { return cols_; }

  // Accessors: return element by row and column.
  T& operator() (size_type row, size_type col) {
    return data_[ index(row, col) ];
  }

  const T& operator() (size_type row, size_type col) const {
    return data_[ index(row, col) ];
  }

private:
  size_type rows_, cols_;
  std::vector<T> data_;

  size_type index(size_type row, size_type col) const {
    SCPP_TEST_ASSERT(row < rows_, "Row " << row
      << " must be less than " << rows_);
    SCPP_TEST_ASSERT(col < cols_, "Column " << col
      << " must be less than " << cols_);
    return cols_ * row + col;
  }
};
```

First of all, there are two constructors. The first allows you to create a matrix with a specified number of rows and columns. The second, with the additional `init_value` argument, allows you also to initialize each element to a specified value (e.g., to set each element of a `matrix<double>` to 0.0). Note that access to elements is provided via the `()` operator, not `[]`. This is because the `[]` operator in C++ takes only one argument, never two or more. So to access a multidimensional array, we either need to use multiple `[]` operators, such as `my_matrix[i][j]`, or a single `()` operator, such as `my_matrix(i,j)`.

The first approach could be achieved if we had the `[]` operator return a `T*` pointer to the zeroth element of the *i*-th row. However, this denies us the diagnosis of a column index out of bounds, which defeats the purpose of catching bugs at runtime. We could, of course, create some template class that would include a smart reference to a row, return an instance of it using the first operator (`[i]`), and then use the bounds check in the second operator (`[j]`). To some degree, it is a matter of taste. I did not see the value of resorting to this complex design just to preserve the `my_matrix[i][j]` syntax, and the `()` operator with multiple arguments seems just fine.

The checks for an index out of bounds are performed inside the `index(row, col)` function, separately for row and column numbers, and in the case of a runtime error lead to calls to an error handler that are familiar by now. Finally, at the end of the same file, you will discover a `<<` operator for a template `matrix<T>`. They are provided so you can output your matrix like this:

```
cout << "my matrix =\n" << my_matrix << endl;
```

as long as the matrix is not too large and the type T defines the `<<` operator.

Rules for this chapter to avoid "index out of bounds" errors:

- Do not use static or dynamically allocated arrays; use a template array or vector instead.
- Do not use `new` and `delete` operators with brackets—leave it up to the template vector to allocate multiple elements.
- Use `scpp:vector` instead of `std::vector` and `scpp::array` consistently instead of a static array, and switch the sanity checks on.
- For a multidimensional array, use `scpp::matrix` and access elements through the () operator to provide index-out-of-bounds checks.

CHAPTER 5

Pointer Arithmetic

The pointer arithmetic that C++ inherited from C allows you to calculate any value whatsoever, use it as a pointer (to `int`, `double`, or any other type) and read from that portion of memory—or even worse, write into it. Actually, pointer arithmetic is just another syntax to access memory the way an index does in the array, and the consequences are exactly the same, as discussed in Chapter 4. The difference is that, in case of a vector accessed via an index, we can write our own [ ] operator with a sanity check, whereas in pointer arithmetic we cannot.

Therefore, the advice here is very simple: *do not use pointer arithmetic*. There is nothing you can do with it that you cannot do with a vector and an index. In fact, in Chapter 6 we'll see that sometimes indexes work where pointers don't. So avoid pointer arithmetic. It is evil.

Rule for this chapter to avoid errors in pointer arithmetic:

- Avoid pointer arithmetic. Use template vector or array with index instead.

Invalid Pointers, References, and Iterators

Consider the following code example:

```
vector<int> v;

// Add some elements
for(int i=0; i<10; ++i)
  v.push_back(i);

int* my_favorite_element_ptr = &v[3];
cout << "My favorite element = " << (*my_favorite_element_ptr) << endl;
cout << "Its address = " <<  my_favorite_element_ptr  << endl;

cout << "Adding more elements..."<< endl;

// Adding more elements
for(int i=0; i<100; ++i)
  v.push_back(i*10);

cout << "My favorite element = " << (*my_favorite_element_ptr) << endl;
cout << "Its address = " <<  &v[3]  << endl;
```

What's going on here? We create a vector containing 10 elements, and for some reason decide to save for later a pointer to element with index 3. Then we add more elements to the vector and try to reuse the pointer we've acquired before. What is wrong with this code? Let's look at the output it produces:

```
My favorite element = 3 Its address = 0x1001000cc
Adding more elements
...
My favorite element = 3
Its address = 0x10010028c
```

Note that after we add more elements to the vector, the address of the element &v[3] has changed! The problem is that when we add new elements to the vector, the existing elements might move to a totally different location.

Here is how such code works. When we create a vector, it allocates by default some number of elements (usually about 16). Then if we try to add more elements than the capacity allows, the vector allocates a new, larger array, copies existing elements from the old location to a new one, and continues to add new elements until the new capacity is exceeded. The old memory is deallocated, and might be reused for other purposes.

Meanwhile, our pointer still points to the old location, which is now in the deallocated memory. So what would happen if we continue to use it? If no one has reused that memory yet, we might get "lucky" and not notice anything, as in the example above. Even in this best-case scenario, though, if we write (assign a value) into that location, it will not change the value of the element v[3] because it is already located elsewhere.

If we are less lucky and that memory was reused for some other purpose, the consequences could be pretty bad, ranging from changing an unrelated variable that was unlucky enough to occupy the same place, to a core dump.

The preceding example deals with a pointer. The exact same thing happens when you do it using a reference; for example, instead of:

```
int* my_favorite_element_ptr = &v[3];
```

suppose one writes:

```
int& my_favorite_element_ref = v[3];
```

The result would be exactly the same. The reason is that the reference is just a "dereferenced pointer." It knows the address of a variable, but does not require an asterisk in front of the variable to reach the memory to which it points. So the syntax is different, but the result is the same.

And finally, the same thing is true when we use iterators. Consider the following example:

```
vector<int> v;

for(int i=0; i<10; ++i)
  v.push_back(i);

vector<int>::const_iterator old_begin = v.begin();

cout << "Adding more elements … "<< endl;

for(int i=0; i<100; ++i)
  v.push_back(i*10);

vector<int>::const_iterator new_begin = v.begin();
if(old_begin == new_begin)
  cout << "Begin-s are the same." << endl;
else
  cout << "Begin-s are DIFFERENT." << endl;
```

As you have probably already guessed, the output of this program is:

```
Adding more elements ...

Begin-s are DIFFERENT.
```

So if you were holding an iterator to some element (any element, not necessarily the one to which `begin()` points), it might be invalid after changing the contents of the vector because the internal array, and correspondingly the iterator `begin()`, might have moved to some other place.

Therefore, any pointers, references, or iterators pointing to the elements of a vector obtained before modifying the vector should not be used after one modifies the vector by adding new elements. Actually, the same is true for almost all STL containers and all operations modifying the size of the container, e.g., adding or removing elements. Some containers, such as `hash_set` and `hash_map`, do not formally belong to the STL, but they are STL-like, will probably be part of STL soon, and behave the same way as STL containers in the situation discussed in here: the iterators become invalid after modifying a container. And even if you are using an STL container that would preserve the iterator to its element after the addition or removal of some other elements, the whole spirit of the STL library is that one could replace one container with another and the code should continue to work. So it is a good idea not to assume that the iterators are still valid after any STL or STL-like container is modified.

Note that in the previous example we modified the container inside the same thread we used to access the pointer. The same and even more problems could be created if you hold a pointer, reference, or iterator in one thread while modifying the container from another thread, but as mentioned in the Preface, the discussion of multithreading is outside the scope of this book.

Interestingly, in the preceding example, the index would work where the pointer failed: if you have marked your element by holding a zero-based index to it (in the first example, something like `int index_of_my_favorite_element = 3`), the example would continue to work correctly. Of course, using an index is slightly more expensive (slower) than using a pointer because in order to access an element corresponding to this index, a vector must do some arithmetic, i.e., calculate the address of the variable every time you use the `[]` operator. The advantage is that it works. The disadvantage is that it works only for vectors. For all other STL containers, once you've modified the container, you must find the iterator pointing to the element you need again.

Rule for this chapter to avoid errors with invalid pointers, references, and iterators:

- Do not hold pointers, references, or iterators to the element of a container after you've modified the container.

CHAPTER 7

Uninitialized Variables

Various errors can occur when adding variables to complex classes and using them as arguments. This chapter shows you a simple way to avoid such errors.

Initialized Numbers (int, double, etc.)

Imagine that you have a class named MyClass with several constructors. Suppose you've decided to add some new data member named int_data_ to the private section of this class:

```
class MyClass {
 public:
  MyClass()
  : int_data_(0)
  {}

  explicit MyClass(const Apple& apple)
  : int_data_(0)
  {}

  MyClass(const string& some_text, double weight)
  : int_data_(0), some_text_(some_text)
  {}


 private:
  int int_data_;
  std::string some_text_;
};
```

When adding the new data member, you have a lot of work to do. Every time you add a new data member *of a built-in type*, do not forget to initialize it in every constructor like this: int_data_(0). But wait! If you read the Preface to this book, you probably remember that we are not supposed to say "Every time you do A, don't forget to do B." Indeed, this is an error-prone approach. If you forget to initialize this data member, it will most likely fill with garbage that would depend on the previous history of the computer and the application, and will create strange and hard-to-reproduce behavior. So what should we do to prevent such problems?

Before we answer this question, let's first discuss why it's only relevant for built-in types. Let's take a look at the data member some_text_, which is of the type std::string. When you add a data member some_text_ to the class MyClass, you do not necessarily need to add its initialization to every constructor of MyClass, because if you don't do it, the default constructor of the std::string will be called for you automatically by the compiler and will initialize the some_text_ to a reproducible state (in this case, an empty string). But the built-in types do not have constructors—that's the problem. Therefore, the solution is simple: for class data members, do not use built-in types, use classes:

- Instead of int, use Int
- Instead of unsigned, use Unsigned
- Instead of double, use Double

and so on. The complete source code of these classes can be found in Appendix F in the file named *scpp_types.hpp*. Let's take a look. The core of this code is the template class TNumber:

```cpp
template <typename T>
class TNumber {
 public:
  TNumber(const T& x=0)
    : data_(x)
  {}

  operator T () const { return data_; }

  TNumber& operator = (const T& x) {
    data_ = x;
    return *this;
  }

  // postfix operator x++
  TNumber operator ++ (int) {
    TNumber<T> copy(*this);
    ++data_;
    return copy;
  }

  // prefix operator ++x
  TNumber& operator ++ () {
    ++data_;
    return *this;
  }

  TNumber& operator += (T x) {
    data_ += x;
    return *this;
  }
```

```
  TNumber& operator -= (T x) {
    data_ -= x;
    return *this;
  }

  TNumber& operator *= (T x) {
    data_ *= x;
    return *this;
  }

  TNumber& operator /= (T x) {
    SCPP_TEST_ASSERT(x!=0, "Attempt to divide by 0");
    data_ /= x;
    return *this;
  }

  T operator / (T x) {
    SCPP_TEST_ASSERT(x!=0, "Attempt to divide by 0");
    return data_ / x;
  }

private:
  T data_;
};
```

First of all, the constructor taking type T (where T is any built-in type, e.g., int, double, float, etc.) is not declared with the keyword explicit. This is intentional. The next function defined in the class is operator T (), which allows an implicit conversion of an instance of this class back into its corresponding built-in type. This class is intentionally designed to make it easy to convert the built-in types into it and back. It defines several common operators that you would expect to use with a built-in numeric type.

And finally, here are the definitions of actual types we can use:

```
typedef    TNumber<int>         Int;
typedef    TNumber<unsigned>    Unsigned;
typedef    TNumber<int64>       Int64;
typedef    TNumber<unsigned64>  Unsigned64;
typedef    TNumber<float>       Float;
typedef    TNumber<double>      Double;
typedef    TNumber<char>        Char;
```

How do you use these new types, such as Int and Double, with names that look like built-in types but start with uppercase letters? All these types work exactly the same way as the corresponding built-in types with one difference: they each have a default constructor, and it initializes them to zero. As a result, in the example of the class MyClass you can write:

```
class MyClass{
public:
  MyClass()
  {}
```

```
  explicit MyClass(const Apple& apple)
  {}

  MyClass(const string& some_text, double weight)
  : some_text_(some_text)
  {}

 private:
  Int int_data_;
  std::string some_text_;
};
```

The variable int_data_ here is declared as Int, with an uppercase first letter, not int, and as a result you don't have to put an initialization of it in all the constructors. It will be automatically initialized to zero.

Actually, there is one more difference: when you use built-in types, an attempt to divide by zero can lead to different consequences depending on the compiler and OS. In our case, for the sake of consistency, this runtime error will lead to a call to the same error handler function as we've used for other errors, so that you can debug on error (see Chapter 15).

 Robust code should not refer to variables before initializing them, but it is considered a good practice to have a safe value such as 0 instead of garbage in an uninitialized variable in case the code does refer to it.

Uninitialized Boolean

But haven't we forgotten one more built-in type specific to C++— type bool (i.e., Boolean)? No, it is just a special case, because for a Boolean we do not need operators such as ++. Instead, we need specifically Boolean operators, such as &= and |=, so this type is defined separately:

```
class Bool {
 public:
  Bool(bool x=false)
  : data_(x)
  {}

  operator bool () const { return data_; }

  Bool& operator = (bool x) {
    data_ = x;
    return *this;
  }

  Bool& operator &= (bool x) {
    data_ &= x;
    return *this;
  }
```

```
  Bool& operator |= (bool x) {
    data_ |= x;
    return *this;
  }

 private:
  bool data_;
};

inline
std::ostream& operator << (std::ostream& os, Bool b) {
  if(b)
    os << "True";
  else
    os << "False";
  return os;
}
```

Again, as with the other classes wrapping built-in types, the type Bool (uppercase) behaves exactly like bool (the original built-in type), with two exceptions:

- It is initialized to false.
- It has a << operator that prints False and True instead of 0 and 1, which leads to much clearer, human-readable messages.

Why is it initialized to false, not to true? Maybe because the author is a pessimist, but you can easily follow the pattern and create a new class like BoolOptimistic that is initialized by default to true.

The only thing that we have yet to initialize is a pointer, which naturally should be initialized by default to NULL. We'll deal with this later in Chapter 9.

So far, the motivation for using classes Int, Unsigned, Double, etc., instead of the corresponding lowercase built-in types was that you can skip initialization in multiple constructors. If you use them more widely, say, for passing arguments to the functions, here is what will to happen. Suppose you have a function taking an unsigned (the built-in one):

```
void SomeFunctionTaking_unsigned(unsigned u);
```

then the following will compile:

```
int i = 0;
SomeFunctionTaking_unsigned(i);
```

Not so with the classes we've discussed. If we have a function:

```
void SomeFunctionTakingUnsigned(Unsigned u);
```

then the following does not compile:

```
Int i = 0;
SomeFunctionTakingUnsigned(i);
```

Therefore, in this case, you get additional type safety at compile time for free.

Rules for this chapter to avoid uninitialized variables, especially data members of a class:

- Do not use built-in types such as `int`, `unsigned`, `double`, `bool`, etc., for class data members. Instead, use `Int`, `Unsigned`, `Double`, `Bool`, etc., because you will not need to initialize them in constructors.
- Use these new classes instead of built-in types for passing parameters to functions, to get additional type safety.

CHAPTER 8

Memory Leaks

By definition, a memory leak is a situation where we allocate some memory from the heap—in C++ by using the new operator, and in C by using malloc() or calloc()—then assign the address of this memory to a pointer, and somehow lose this value either by letting the pointer go out of scope:

```
{
  MyClass* my_class_object = new MyClass;
  DoSomething(my_class_object);
} // memory leak!!!
```

or by assigning some other value to it:

```
MyClass* my_class_object = new MyClass;
DoSomething(my_class_object);
my_class_object = NULL; // memory leak!!!
```

There are also situations when programmers keep allocating new memory and do not lose any pointers to it, but keep pointers to objects that the program is not going to use anymore. The latter is not formally a memory leak, but leads to the same situation: a program running out of memory. We'll leave the latter error to the attention of the programmer, and concentrate on the first one—the "formal" memory leak.

Consider two objects containing pointers to each other (Figure 8-1). This situation is known as a "circular reference." Pointers exist to A and to B, but if there are no other pointers to at least one of these objects from somewhere else, there is no way to reclaim the memory for either variable and therefore you create a memory leak. These two objects will live happily ever after and will never be destroyed. Now consider the opposite example. Suppose we have a class with a method that can be run in a separate thread:

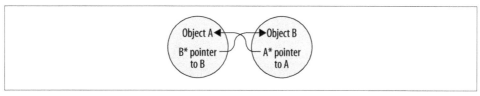

Figure 8-1. Circular references

```
class SelfResponsible : public Thread {
public:
  virtual void Run() {
    DoSomethingImportantAndCommitSuicide();
  }

  void DoSomethingImportantAndCommitSuicide() {
    sleep(1000);
    delete this;
  }
};
```

We start its Run() method in a separate thread like this:

```
Thread* my_object = new SelfResponsible;
my_object->Start();  // call method Run() in a separate thread
my_object = NULL;
```

After that we assign NULL to the pointer and lose the address of this object, thus creating a memory leak according to the definition at the beginning of this chapter. However, if we look inside the DoSomethingImportantAndCommitSuicide() method, we'll see that after doing something the object will delete itself, thus releasing this memory back to the heap to be reused. So this is not actually a memory leak.

Considering all these examples, a better definition of a memory leak is as follows. If we allocate memory (using the new operator), someone or something (some object) must be responsible for:

- deleting this memory;
- doing it the right way (using the correct delete operator, with or without brackets);
- doing it exactly once;
- and preferably doing it ASAP after we are done using this memory.

This responsibility for deleting the memory is usually called *ownership* of the object. In the previous example, the object took ownership of itself. So to summarize, a memory leak is a situation where the ownership of allocated memory is lost.

Consider the following code:

```
void SomeFunction() {
  MyClass* my_class_object = NULL;

  // some code …
```

```
if(SomeCondition1()) {
  my_class_object = new MyClass;
}

// more code

if(SomeCondition2()) {
  DoSomething(my_class_object);
  delete my_class_object;
  return;
}

// even more code

if(SomeCondition3()) {
  DoSomethingElse(my_class_object);
  delete my_class_object;
  return;
}

delete my_class_object;
return;
}
```

The reason we've started with the NULL pointer is to avoid the question of why we don't just create the object on the stack and avoid the whole problem of deallocating it altogether. There can be multiple reasons for not creating an object on the stack. Sometimes the creation of an object must be delayed to a point in the program later than when the variable holding the memory is created; or it might be created by some other factory class and what we get is a pointer returned to us together with responsibility to delete it when we are done using it; or maybe we don't know whether we will create the object at all, as in the previous example.

Now that we have an object created on the heap, we are responsible for deleting it. What is wrong with the preceding code? Obviously, it is *fragile*: i.e., every time we modify it by adding an additional `return` statement, we must delete the object just before returning. In this example, the responsibility to delete the object lies with the programmer. This is error-prone, and therefore against the principle declared in the Preface.

But even if we remember to delete the object before each return statement, this does not solve our problems. If any of the functions called from this code could throw an exception, then it actually means that we might "return" from any line of code containing a function call. Thus, we must surround the code with try-catch statements and, if we catch an exception, remember to delete the object and then throw a further exception. This seems like lots of work just to avoid a memory leak. The code becomes more crowded with statements dealing with cleanup and therefore becomes less readable, and the programmer has less time to concentrate on actual work.

The solution to this problem, widely known in C++ literature, is to use *smart pointers*. These are template classes that behave like normal pointers (or sometimes not exactly like normal pointers) but that take ownership of the objects assigned to them, leaving the programmer with no further worries. In this case, the function shown earlier would look like this:

```
void SomeFunction() {
  SmartPointer<MyClass> my_class_object;

  // some code …

  if(SomeCondition1()) {
    my_class_object = new MyClass;
  }

  // more code

  if(SomeCondition2()) {
    DoSomething(my_class_object);
    return;
  }

  // even more code

  if(SomeCondition3()) {
    DoSomethingElse(my_class_object);
    return;
  }

  return;
}
```

Note that we do not delete the allocated object anywhere. It is now the responsibility of the smart pointer, my_class_object.

This is actually a special case of a more general C++ pattern where some resource is acquired by an object (usually in a constructor, but not necessarily) and then this object is responsible for releasing the resource and will do so in a destructor. One example of using this pattern is obtaining a lock on a Mutex object when entering a function:

```
void MyClass::MyMethod() {
  MutexLock lock(&my_mutex_);
  // some code
} // destructor ~MutexLock() is called here releasing my_mutex_
```

In this case, the MyClass class has a data member named my_mutex_ that must be obtained at the beginning of a method and released before leaving the method. It is obtained by MutexLock in the constructor and automatically released in its destructor, so we can be sure that no matter what happens inside the code of the MyClass::MyMethod() function —in particular, how many return statements we might insert or whatever might throw an exception—the method won't forget to release my_mutex_ before returning.

Now let's return to the problem of memory leaks. The solution is that whenever we allocate new memory, we must immediately assign the pointer to that memory to some smart pointer. We now do not have to worry about deleting the memory; that responsibility is given to the smart pointer.

At this point you might ask the following questions regarding the smart pointer class:

1. Are you allowed to copy a smart pointer?
2. If yes, which one of the multiple copies of the smart pointer is responsible for deleting the object they all point to?
3. Does the smart pointer represent a pointer to an object or an array of objects (i.e., does it use the `delete` operator with or without brackets)?
4. Does a smart pointer correspond to a `const` pointer or a non-`const` pointer?

Depending on the answers to these questions, you could come up with a rather large number of different smart pointers. And indeed, there are a great many of them discussed and used in the C++ community and provided by different libraries, most notably, the *boost* library. However, in my opinion the multitude of different smart pointer types creates new opportunities for errors, for example, assigning a pointer pointing to an object to a smart pointer that expects an array (i.e., would use a `delete` with brackets) or vice versa.

One of the smart pointers—`auto_ptr<T>`—has the strange property that when you have an auto pointer `p1` and then make a copy of it `p2` as follows:

```
auto_ptr<int> p1(new int);
auto_ptr<int> p2(p1);
```

the pointer `p1` becomes NULL, which I find counterintuitive and therefore error-prone.

In my experience, there are two smart pointer classes that have so far covered all my needs in preventing memory leaks:

1. The reference counting pointer (a.k.a. the shared pointer)
2. The scoped pointer

The difference between the two is that the reference counting pointer can be copied and the scoped pointer cannot. However, the scoped pointer is more efficient.

We'll look at each of these in the following sections.

Reference Counting Pointers

As mentioned above, the reference counting pointer can be copied. As a result, several copies of a smart pointer could point to the same object. This leads to the question of which copy is responsible for deleting the object that they all point to. The answer is that the last smart pointer of the group to die will delete the object it points to. It's analogous to the household rule: "the last person to leave the room will switch the lights off."

To implement this algorithm, the pointers share a counter that keeps track of how many smart pointers refer to the same object—hence the term "reference counting." Reference counts are used in a wide range of situations: the term simply means that the implementation has a hidden integer variable that serves as a counter. Each time someone creates a new copy of a smart pointer that points to the target object, the implementation increments the counter; when any smart pointer is deleted, the implementation decrements the counter. So the target object will be around as long as it's needed, but no longer that that.

An implementation of reference counting pointers is provided by my library in the file *scpp_refcountptr.hpp*. Here's the public portion of this class:

```cpp
template < typename T>
class RefCountPtr {
 public:

  explicit RefCountPtr(T* p = NULL) {
    Create(p);
  }

  RefCountPtr(const RefCountPtr<T>& rhs) {
    Copy(rhs);
  }

  RefCountPtr<T>& operator=(const RefCountPtr<T>& rhs) {
    if(ptr_ != rhs.ptr_)
    {
      Kill();
      Copy(rhs);
    }

    return *this;
  }

  RefCountPtr<T>& operator=(T* p) {
    if(ptr_ != p) {
      Kill();
      Create(p);
    }

    return *this;
  }

  ~RefCountPtr() {
    Kill();
  }

  T* Get()const { return ptr_; }

  T* operator->() const {
    SCPP_TEST_ASSERT(ptr_ != NULL,
      "Attempt to use operator -> on NULL pointer.");
    return ptr_;
  }
```

```
    T& operator* ()const {
      SCPP_TEST_ASSERT(ptr_ != NULL,
        "Attempt to use operator * on NULL pointer.");
      return *ptr_;
    }
```

Note that both the copy-constructor and assignment operators are provided, so one could copy these pointers. In this case, both the original pointer and the copied one point to the same object (or to NULL, if the original pointer was NULL). In this sense they behave the same way as the regular "raw" T* pointers. If you no longer need to use the object, you can "kill" the reference counting pointer by assigning NULL to it.

There are a couple of problems with the reference counting pointer. First, creating one with a non-NULL argument is expensive, because the implementation uses the new operator to allocate an integer on heap, a relatively slow operation. Second, of course, the reference counting pointer is not multithread-safe. I've declared that discussions of multithreading are beyond the scope of this book, but here it's important enough to mention. Let's concentrate on the previous problem—the cost of using a reference counting pointer. You can use it when you are sure that you will need to copy it, and when you can be reasonably sure that the cost of creating one is negligible compared to the execution time of the rest of your code.

Scoped Pointers

In cases when you don't plan on copying the smart pointer and just want to make sure that the allocated resource will be deallocated properly, as in the earlier examples of the SomeFunction() method, there is a much simpler solution: the scoped pointer. Let's take a look at its code provided in the file *scpp_scopedptr.hpp*:

```
template <typename T>
class ScopedPtr {
 public:

  explicit ScopedPtr(T* p = NULL)
  : ptr_(p)
  {}

  ScopedPtr<T>& operator=(T* p) {
    if(ptr_ != p) {
      delete ptr_;
      ptr_ = p;
    }

    return *this;
  }

  ~ScopedPtr() {
    delete ptr_;
  }
```

```
    T* Get() const {
      return ptr_;
    }

    T* operator->() const {
      SCPP_TEST_ASSERT(ptr_ != NULL,
        "Attempt to use operator -> on NULL pointer.");
      return ptr_;
    }

    T& operator* () const {
      SCPP_TEST_ASSERT(ptr_ != NULL,
        "Attempt to use operator * on NULL pointer.");
      return *ptr_;
    }

    // Release ownership of the object to the caller.
    T* Release() {
      T* p = ptr_;
      ptr_ = NULL;
      return p;
    }

  private:
    T*  ptr_;

    // Copy is prohibited:
    ScopedPtr(const ScopedPtr<T>& rhs);
    ScopedPtr<T>& operator=(const ScopedPtr<T>& rhs);
};
```

Again, the most important property of this class for us is that its destructor deletes the object it points to (if it is not NULL, of course). The difference between usage of the scoped pointer and the reference counter pointer is that the scoped pointer cannot be copied. Both the copy-constructor and assignment operator are declared private, so any attempt to copy this pointer will not compile. This removes the need to count how many copies of the same smart pointer point to the same object—there is always only one, and therefore this pointer does not allocate an int from the heap to count its copies. For this reason, it is as fast as a pointer can be.

You have also probably noticed that in both RefCountPtr and ScopedPtr we diagnose an attempt to dereference the NULL pointer. We'll talk more about this in the next chapter.

As you'll recall from Chapter 4 concerning arrays, we have discussed which of the two new operators to use: the one without brackets. As for the corresponding delete operators, we should use *neither*. Do not delete the objects yourself; leave it to smart pointers.

Enforcing Ownership with Smart Pointers

Now let's discuss potential errors when using functions that return pointers. Suppose, we have a function that returns a pointer to some type `MyClass`:

```
MyClass* MyFactoryClass::Create(const Inputs& inputs);
```

The very first question about this function is whether the caller of this function is responsible for deleting this object, or is this a pointer to an instance of `MyClass` that the instance of `MyFactoryClass` owns? This should of course be documented in a comment in the header file where this function is declared, but the reality of the software world is that it rarely is. But even if the author of the function did provide a comment that the function creates a new object on the heap and the caller is responsible for deleting it, we now find ourselves saying that every time we receive a pointer to an object from a function call, we need to remember to check the comments (or in the absence of a comment—the code itself if available) to find out whether we are responsible for deleting this object. And as we have decided in the Preface, we would prefer to rely on a compiler rather than on a programmer. Therefore, a fool-proof way to enforce the ownership of the object is for the function to return a smart pointer. For example:

```
RefCountPtr<MyClass> MyFactoryClass::Create(const Inputs& inputs);
```

Not only does this design leave no doubt about the ownership of the object returned by the function, it leaves no opportunity for a memory leak. On the other hand, if you find the reference counting pointer too slow for your purposes, you might want to return a scoped pointer. But there is one problem: the `ScopedPtr<MyClass>` cannot be copied, and therefore it cannot be returned in a traditional way:

```
ScopedPtr<MyClass> MyFactoryClass::Create(const Inputs& inputs) {
  ScopedPTr<MyClass> result(new MyClass(inputs));
  return result; // Won't compile !
}
```

Therefore, the way around the problem is to do this:

```
ScopedPtr<MyClass> result;  // Create an empty scoped pointer
// Fill it:
void MyFactoryClass::Create(const Inputs& inputs, ScopedPtr<MyClass>& result);
```

Here you create a scoped pointer containing NULL and give it to `MyFactoryClass::Create()` to fill it up. This approach again leaves no room for mistakes regarding the ownership of the object created by the function. If you are not sure which of the two pointers to return, you can either:

- Return the faster `ScopedPtr` and then use its `Release()` method to transfer ownership to a `RefCountPtr` if necessary.
- Provide both methods.

There is also an opposite situation when the `SomeClass::Find()` method returns a pointer to an object but the user does not have ownership of it:

```
// Returns a pointer to a result, caller DOES NOT OWN the result.
MyClass* SomeClass::Find(const Inputs& inputs);
```

In this case, the pointer returned by this function points to an object that belongs to something inside the `SomeClass` object.

The first problem here is that the `SomeClass` object thinks that it is responsible for deleting the `MyClass` instance to which it just returned a pointer, and therefore it will delete it at some point in the future. In this case, if the user of this function will delete the pointer he received, this instance will be deleted more than once, which is not a good idea. Second, this instance might be part of an array of `MyClass` objects that is created inside, say, a template vector using operator `new[]` (with brackets), and we are now trying to delete an object from that array using operator `delete` without brackets. This is also not good. Finally, the instance of `MyClass` could be created on stack, and should not ever be deleted using operator `delete` at all.

In this case, any attempt to delete this object that we do not own—directly or by assigning it to a smart pointer of any kind that would take ownership of it—would lead to disaster. An appropriate way of returning this pointer is to return a "semi-smart" pointer that does not own the object it points to. This will be discussed in the next chapter.

Rules for this chapter to avoid memory leaks:

- Every time you create an object using the `new` operator, immediately assign the result to a smart pointer (reference counting point or scoped pointer is recommended).

- Use the `new` operator only without brackets. If you need to create an array, create a new template vector, which is a single object.

- Avoid circular references.

- When writing a function returning a pointer, return a smart pointer instead of a raw one, to enforce the ownership of the result.

CHAPTER 9

Dereferencing NULL Pointers

One of the most frequent reasons for program crashes (a.k.a. core dumps under Unix) is an attempt to dereference a NULL pointer. As we saw in the previous chapter, both smart pointers discussed there—the RefCountPtr and the ScopedPtr—have run-time diagnostics for that. However, not every pointer is a smart pointer that has ownership of some object. To diagnose an attempt to dereference a pointer that does not have ownership of an object, I'll introduce here a "semi-smart" pointer that does not delete the object it points to. Let's take a look at the public portion of it in the file *scpp_ptr.hpp*:

```cpp
// Template pointer, does not take ownership of an object.
template <typename T>
class Ptr {
 public:

  explicit Ptr(T* p=NULL)
  : ptr_(p) {
  }

  T* Get() const {
    return ptr_;
  }

  Ptr<T>& operator=(T* p) {
    ptr_ = p;
    return *this;
  }

  T* operator->() const {
    SCPP_TEST_ASSERT(ptr_ != NULL,
      "Attempt to use operator -> on NULL pointer.");
    return ptr_;
  }

  T& operator* () const {
    SCPP_TEST_ASSERT(ptr_ != NULL,
      "Attempt to use operator * on NULL pointer.");
    return *ptr_;
  }
```

Despite the presence of operator=, this is not an assignment operator that would tell the compiler what to do when we try to assign one Ptr<T> to another. The assignment operator for this class, if we had writthen one, would be declared as:

```
Ptr<T>& operator=(const Ptr<T>& that);
```

Note that the operator= declared in the preceding class has a different signature: it includes a raw pointer p on the right side. Therefore, this class leaves it up to the compiler to create both the copy constructor and the assignment operator of the Ptr<T>. Because both the copy constructor and assignment operators for the Ptr<T> class are allowed, you are free to copy these pointers, return them from functions, and so on.

At this point you might ask: if we are advised to use Ptr<T> instead of T*, what should we use for a const T* pointer? The answer is easy: Ptr<const T>. Suppose you have a class:

```
class MyClass {
 public:
  explicit MyClass(int id)
  : id_(id) {}

  int GetId() const { return id_; }
  void SetId(int id) { id_ = id; }

 private:
  int id_;
};
```

If you want to create a semi-smart pointer that behaves like const MyClass*, all you have to do is write:

```
scpp::Ptr<const MyClass> p(new MyClass(1));
cout << "Id = " << p->GetId() << endl;  // Compiles and runs.
p->SetId(666); //    Does not compile!
```

Note that an attempt to call a non-const function on this pointer does not compile, which means that it correctly reproduces the behavior of a const pointer.

The Ptr<T> template pointer has the following features:

1. It does not take ownership of the object it points to, and should be used as a replacement for a raw pointer in the same situation.
2. It is by default initialized to NULL (thus following the spirit of Chapter 7).
3. It offers run-time diagnostics of an attempt to dereference itself when it is NULL.

Rules for this chapter to catch attempts to dereference a NULL pointer:

- If you have a pointer that owns the object it points to, use a smart pointer (a reference counting pointer or scoped pointer).
- When you have a raw pointer T* pointing to an object you do not own, use the template class Ptr<T> instead.
- For a const pointer (i.e., const T*) use Ptr<const T>.

CHAPTER 10

Copy Constructors and Assignment Operators

Suppose you have a class `MyClass` that looks something like this:

```
class MyClass {
 public:
  // Constructors

  // Copy-constructor
  MyClass(const MyClass& that)
  : int_data_(that.int_data_),
    dbl_data_(that.dbl_data_),
    str_data_(that.str_data_) {
  }

  // Assignment operator
  MyClass& operator = (const MyClass& that) {
    if(this != &that) {
      int_data_ = that.int_data_;
      dbl_data_ = that.dbl_data_;
      str_data_ = that.str_data_;
    }
    return *this;
  }

  // Some other methods here
 private:
  Int int_data_;
  Double dbl_data_;
  string str_data_;
  // Each time you add a new data member in here,
  // do not forget to add corresponding code to the
  // copy-constructor and assignment operators!
};
```

What is wrong with this class? It is summarized in the comment at the end of the private section. You'll remember from the Preface that if we find ourselves saying this, we open up the code to errors and should consider alternatives. And indeed, if you don't write a copy-constructor or assignment operator, C++ will write a "default version" for you. The default version of the copy-constructor of your class will call copy-constructors for all data members (or simply copy the built-in types), and the default version of an assignment operator will call assignment operators for each data member or simply copy the built-in types.

Because of that, the copy constructor and the assignment operator in the previous example are totally unnecessary. Even worse, they are a potential source of errors because they make your code fragile, i.e., it might break if someone tries to modify it. Therefore, in this case it is a good idea to avoid writing copy-constructors and assignment operators altogether.

In general, regarding these two functions, you have the following choices:

- Rely on default versions created for you automatically by a compiler.
- Prohibit copies of any kind by declaring the copy constructor and assignment operator as private, and do not provide an implementation.
- Write your own versions.

For the reasons just discussed, avoid the last option as much as possible. If you find yourself writing copy constructors and assignment operators for some class, ask yourself whether it is really necessary. Maybe you can avoid doing it and switch to the first option (using default versions created by compiler) or use some other methods, such as smart pointers. If you are not sure, use the second option—if there is no copying of any kind, there is no way to make errors. However, be aware that some types of usage of your class (e.g., in `vector<MyClass>`) require a copy constructor and an assignment operator, so prohibiting copies of any kind should be used sparingly, with the understanding that it limits your options when using your class.

Rules for this chapter to avoid errors in copy-constructors and assignment operators:

- Whenever possible, avoid writing a copy-constructor or assignment operator for your classes.
- If the default versions do not work for you, consider prohibiting the copying of instances of your class by declaring the copy-constructor and assignment operator private.

CHAPTER 11

Avoid Writing Code in Destructors

In the previous chapter, we discussed why you should try to avoid writing copy constructors and assignment operators at all. In this chapter we discuss why you should avoid writing code in the destructor. I am not saying that the destructor method should not exist, just that if you do write one, it's a good idea to design your class so that the destructor is empty. The following is acceptable:

```
virtual ~MyClass() {}
```

We will use the term *an empty destructor* when talking about a destructor that has no code inside the curly brackets.

There are several reasons why you might need to write a destructor:

- In a base class, you might want to declare it virtual, so that you can use a pointer to the base class to point to an instance of a derived class.
- In a derived class, you do not have to declare it virtual, but might like to do so for the sake of readability.
- You might need to declare that the destructor does not throw any exceptions.

Let's consider the last reason more closely. It is widely accepted in the C++ literature that throwing exceptions from a destructor is a bad idea. This is because destructors are often called when an exception is already thrown, and throwing a second one during this process would lead to the termination (or crash) of your program, which is probably not your intention. Therefore, in some classes, destructors are declared as follows (this example comes from the file *scpp_assert.hpp*):

```
virtual ~ScppAssertFailedException() throw () {}
```

which means that we promise not to throw an exception from this destructor.

So you can see that it is necessary from time to time to write a destructor. Now let us discuss why it should be an empty one. When would you need any non-trivial code in the destructor? Only if you have acquired, in the constructor or some other method of your class, some resource that you need to release when the object goes away, such as in the following example:

```
class PersonDescription {
 public:
  PersonDescription(const char* first_name, const char* last_name)
  : first_name_(NULL), last_name_(NULL) {
    if(first_name != NULL)
      first_name_ = new string(first_name);

    if(last_name != NULL)
      last_name_ = new string(last_name);
  }

  ~PersonDescription() {
    delete first_name_;
    delete last_name_;
  }

 private:
  PersonDescription(const PersonDescription&);
  PersonDescription& operator=(const PersonDescription&);

  string* first_name_;
  string* last_name_;
};
```

The design of this class violates everything we have discussed in earlier chapters. First of all, we see that every time we might need to add a new element of a person's description, such as a middle name, we would need to remember to add a corresponding cleanup to the destructor, which is a violation of our "do not force the programmer to remember things" principle. A much better design would be:

```
class PersonDescription {
 public:
  PersonDescription(const char* first_name, const char* last_name) {
    if(first_name != NULL)
      first_name_ = new string(first_name);

    if(last_name != NULL)
      last_name_ = new string(last_name);
  }

 private:
  PersonDescription(const PersonDescription&);
  PersonDescription& operator=(const PersonDescription&);

  scpp::ScopedPtr<string> first_name_;
  scpp::ScopedPtr<string> last_name_;
};
```

In this case, we don't need to write a destructor at all because the one generated for us automatically by the compiler will do the job, and this leads to less fragile code while doing less work. However, this is not the main reason for choosing this second type of design. There are more serious potential hazards in the case of the first example.

Suppose we have decided to add sanity checks that the caller has provided the first name and last name:

```cpp
class PersonDescription {
public:
  PersonDescription(const char* first_name, const char* last_name)
  : first_name_(NULL), last_name_(NULL) {
    SCPP_ASSERT(first_name != NULL, "First name must be provided");
    first_name_ = new string(first_name);

    SCPP_ASSERT(last_name != NULL, "Last name must be provided");
    last_name_ = new string(last_name);
  }

  ~PersonDescription() {
    delete first_name_;
    delete last_name_;
  }

private:
  PersonDescription(const PersonDescription&);
  PersonDescription& operator=(const PersonDescription&);

  string* first_name_;
  string* last_name_;
};
```

As we discussed in Part I, our error might not terminate an application, but it might throw an exception. Now we are in trouble: throwing an exception from a constructor could be a bad idea. Let's consider why this is the case. If you are trying to create an object on the stack and the constructor does its job normally (without throwing an exception), then when the object goes out of scope, the destructor will be called. However, if the constructor did not finish its job because the code of the constructor threw an exception, *the destructor will not be called.*

Therefore, in the preceding example, if we suppose that the first name was supplied but the second was not, the string for the first name will be allocated but never deleted, and thus we will have a memory leak. However, all is not lost. Let's look a little deeper into this situation. If we have an object that contains other objects, an important question is: exactly which destructors will be called and which will not?

To answer this question, let's conduct a small experiment. Suppose we have the following three classes:

```cpp
class A {
public:
  A() { cout << "Creating A" << endl; }
  ~A() { cout << "Destroying A" << endl; }
};

class B {
public:
  B() { cout << "Creating B" << endl; }
```

```
  ~B() { cout << "Destroying B" << endl; }
};

class C : public A {
 public:
  C() {
    cout << "Creating C" << endl;
    throw "Don't like C";
  }
  ~C() { cout << "Destroying C" << endl; }

 private:
  B b_;
};
```

Note that class C contains class B *by composition* (i.e., we have a data member in C of type B). It also contains the object of type A *by inheritance*: i.e., somewhere inside the object C there is an object A. Now, what happens if the constructor of C throws an exception? The following code example:

```
int main() {
  cout << "Testing throwing from constructor." << endl;
  try {
    C c;
  } catch (…) {
    cout << "Caught an exception" << endl;
  }

  return 0;
}
```

produces this output:

```
Testing throwing from constructor.
Creating A
Creating B
Creating C
Destroying B
Destroying A
Caught an exception
```

Note that it is only the destructor of C that was not executed: the destructors of both A and B were called. So the conclusion is simple and logical: for objects whose constructors are allowed to finish normally, the destructors will be called, even if these objects are part of the larger object constructor that did *not* finish normally. Therefore, let's rewrite our example with sanity checks using smart pointers:

```
class PersonDescription {
public:
  PersonDescription(const char* first_name, const char* last_name) {
    SCPP_ASSERT(first_name != NULL, "First name must be provided");
    first_name_ = new string(first_name);

    SCPP_ASSERT(last_name != NULL, "Last name must be provided");
    last_name_ = new string(last_name);
```

```
    }
private:
  PersonDescription(const PersonDescription&);
  PersonDescription& operator=(const PersonDescription&);

  scpp::ScopedPtr<string> first_name_;
  scpp::ScopedPtr<string> last_name_;
};
```

Even if the second sanity check throws an exception, the destructor of the smart pointer to `first_name_` will still be called and will do its cleanup. In addition, as a free benefit, we don't need to worry about initializing these smart pointers to NULL—that is done automatically. So we see that throwing an exception from a constructor is a potentially dangerous business: the corresponding destructor will not be called, and we might have a problem—*unless the destructor is empty*.

While the C++ community is divided over whether it is a good idea to throw exceptions from constructors, there is a good argument for allowing the constructor to do so. The constructor does not have a return value, so if some of the inputs are wrong, what should we do? One possibility is to just return from the constructor and have a separate class method such as `bool IsValid()`. And each time you create an object, you should not forget to call `my_object.IsValid()` and see the result... and you can see where this is going. Which brings us back to the original choice: if something goes wrong inside the constructor, throw an exception. This means that the corresponding destructor will not be called, but this is acceptable to do if that destructor is empty.

Rule for this chapter: to avoid memory leaks when throwing exceptions from a constructor:

- Design your class in such a way that the destructor is empty.

CHAPTER 12

How to Write Consistent Comparison Operators

If you wrote a new class `MyClass`, you might want sometimes to write expressions like this:

```
MyClass x, y;
  /// some code initializing x and y
  if(x < y) {
    // do something
  } else if (x == y) {
    // do something else
  }
```

Even if you don't need comparison operators (<, <=, etc.) yourself, you might find that someone attempts to use your class with Standard Template Library operations that require you to define these operators. For example, if you try to sort a vector of instances of your class:

```
vector<MyClass> v;
v.push_back(MyClass(3));
v.push_back(MyClass(1));
v.push_back(MyClass(2));

sort(v.begin(), v.end());
```

an attempt to compile this code fills the screen with diagnostics that look like this:

```
/usr/include/c++/4.2.1/bits/stl_heap.h:121: error: no
    match for 'operator<' in '__first.
    __gnu_cxx::__normal_iterator<_Iterator, _Container>::operator+
    [with _Iterator = MyClass*, _Container = std::vector<MyClass,
    std::allocator<MyClass> >](((const ptrdiff_t&)((const
    ptrdiff_t*)(&
    __parent)))).__gnu_cxx::__normal_iterator<_Iterator,
    _Container>::operator* [with _Iterator = MyClass*, _Container =
    std::vector<MyClass, std::allocator<MyClass> >]() <
    __value'
```

Although this output is not easily readable by a human, after some effort one can find in that pile of information the following useful piece: no match for 'operator<'. What the compiler is unhappy about is that the class MyClass does not define a < operator. All you have to do is add to the definition of MyClass:

```
class MyClass {
 public:
  // constructors, etc…
  bool operator < (const MyClass& that) const {
    // some code returning bool
    return my_data_ < that.my_data_;
  }

 private:
  Int my_data_;
```

and the example compiles, runs, and sorts the vector. The same thing happens if you try to use your class in std::set<MyClass> or as a key in std::map<MyClass, AnyOther Class>. While STL is relatively undemanding and in most cases will be satisfied by the definition of only one < operator, there might be cases when you want to define several comparison operators or potentially all of them. For example, suppose you've decided to write a Date class that would encapsulate the calendar date and you expect that other programmers might want to use all kinds of comparisons: date1 >= date2, etc. There are six comparison operators:

```
<
>
<=
>=
==
!=
```

From the point of view of C++, these operators could be written as six totally independent functions, and nothing in C++ prevents you from writing each one any way you like. However, the user of your class MyClass would expect that if instances of this class satisfy the inequality x1 < x2, then it must also be true that x1 <= x2 and that x2 > x1. In other words, there are some logical relations between these operators, and after writing each comparison operator, it would be a good idea to make sure that these relations hold in order to avoid confusion. In fact, no additional work to achieve this is necessary. There is an easy way to kill all six birds with one stone in two steps.

1. In your class, define the following method:

```
class MyClass {
 public:
  // some code…

  // Returns negative int  when *this <  that,
  //          0             when *this == that and
  //          positive int  when *this >  that.
  int CompareTo(const MyClass& that) const;
```

2. Define all six comparison operators by using the following macro inside the public section of your class:

```
SCPP_DEFINE_COMPARISON_OPERATORS(MyClass)
```

I have defined SCPP_DEFINE_COMPARISON_OPERATORS in the file *scpp_types.hpp* as follows:

```
#define SCPP_DEFINE_COMPARISON_OPERATORS(Class)                        \
    bool operator < (const Class& that) const { return CompareTo(that) < 0; } \
    bool operator > (const Class& that) const { return CompareTo(that) > 0; } \
    bool operator ==(const Class& that) const { return CompareTo(that) ==0; } \
    bool operator <=(const Class& that) const { return CompareTo(that) <=0; } \
    bool operator >=(const Class& that) const { return CompareTo(that) >=0; } \
    bool operator !=(const Class& that) const { return CompareTo(that) !=0; }
```

In one long line, this macro defines all six comparison operators for you in a consistent way. In order for this to work, the only thing you need to do is provide the CompareTo() function in your class. If you ever decide to change the definition of what you mean by > or <= for the instances of your class, you can simply edit that function and the rest will behave accordingly while preserving all the relations one would expect between different comparison operators.

Rule for this chapter to avoid errors when writing comparison operators:

- Write a CompareTo() function and use the SCPP_DEFINE_COMPARISON_OPERATORS macro to implement all the comparison operators.

CHAPTER 13

Errors When Using Standard C Libraries

As we discussed in Chapter 1, C++ inherited the C philosophy and its corresponding problems. But that's not all. It also inherited the standard C library, which is unsafe in several ways, and consequently all its associated problems, sometimes leading to unpredictable behavior up to and including program crashes. For the final chapter in this part of the book, we'll discuss the possible dangers that await you when you use some of the functions that programmers frequently depend on in these libraries.

When we try to use the C string libraries declared in *string.h* or functions such as `sprintf()` declared in *stdio.h*, we may face the following problems:

- The functions that take pointers to character arrays (`char *`) crash when given a NULL instead of a pointer to a valid C string (for example, `strlen(NULL)` will crash).

- Some of the functions writing into a buffer might overwrite past the end of the buffer, thus leading to unpredictable application behavior including crashes.

- The safer versions of the same functions will not overwrite the buffer, but will stop writing into a buffer just before it ends, thus silently truncating the result—probably not the behavior one would want.

There are several potential ways to address these problems:

- Provide versions of the functions that do all the necessary sanity checks and treat the NULL pointers the same way as they would handle an empty string (`const char* empty_string = "";`).

- For those applications where the speed of these string operations should not be compromised, provide versions with temporary sanity checks that are active only during testing.

However, the best possible solution to this problem is not to use the C string libraries at all. Use the classes provided by C++ instead. For example:

- Instead of `strlen(my_c_string)`, you can use `my_cpp_string.size()`.

- Instead of `strcpy()`, just copy the strings using `string`'s assignment operator (i.e., =).

To concatenate two strings, two functions in the C library are available. `strcat()` blindly adds a string to the end of an existing string in a buffer without ever knowing where the buffer ends. By contrast, `strncat()` adds no more than the specified number of bytes, which seems like a step in the right direction, but it still does not know anything about the size of the buffer it adds to. The programmer is responsible for allocating the right amount of space and calculating how many bytes to add.

Instead of `strcat()` or `strncat()`, use either:

```
#include <sstream> // ostringstream
#include <string>

  ostringsream buffer;
  buffer << first_string;
  buffer << additional_string;
  string result = buffer.str();
```

or, even shorter:

```
#include <string>

  string result = first_string;
  result += additional_string;
```

Not only are these more readable and safer, they are actually faster for long strings than `strcat()`! There are no buffers to allocate and overwrite.

If you are working with **std::string** and provide a NULL as an argument in a constructor:

```
std::string empty_string(NULL);
```

the program does not crash. Instead it throws an exception with a human-readable (well, almost human-readable) explanation of what happened:

```
basic_string::_S_construct NULL not valid
```

which translates into plain English as "the constructor of std::string found a NULL as an argument where it expected a valid C string."

The rule for this chapter to avoid buffer overflows and crashes when using C string library functions is to avoid using C string libraries.

- They are not safe and sometimes not even as fast as the corresponding C++ classes, such as **std::string** and **std::ostringstream**. Use C++ classes and you will avoid a number of possible errors leading to program crashes or other unpredictable behavior.

PART III

The Joy of Bug Hunting: From Testing to Debugging to Production

In this part, we assume that your code at least partially adheres to the approaches and guidelines discussed in previous chapters. Now we are ready for testing. Here we discuss the testing and debugging strategy for finding and eliminating bugs in the most efficient way possible.

CHAPTER 14

General Testing Principles

Although it is impossible to test code without concrete knowledge of what a particular program does, and how, there are nevertheless some general principles of testing that are useful to follow. Correctly designed and implemented code must produce the right answer when given correct inputs. Furthermore, when given incorrect ones, the program should not silently die, crash, or get stuck, but should diagnose the problem—where, why, and if necessary, when the error happened—and then either gracefully terminate or return to the initial state from which it can process the next input. Testing must include everything from unit tests of each single class, to unit tests of groups of classes working together, to a test of the whole application.

To the extent possible, you should try to create a reproducible test that leads to the same results when repeated. This can be a challenge when dealing with multi-threaded applications, when the timing of events between different threads is an issue, but even in cases like that it is usually possible to convert tests of some parts of the code to a single-threaded mode where the results should be totally deterministic.

In order to test multiple classes, organize them in a hierarchy such that some classes are considered more "basic" than others. In other words, the classes on one level of the hierarchy can make calls only to the classes on the same level or below, not above. Then the sequence of testing is clear. Otherwise, you'll face a chicken-and-egg problem when deciding what to test first. An even better design is when a class at each level uses only classes below it, as shown in Figure 14-1.

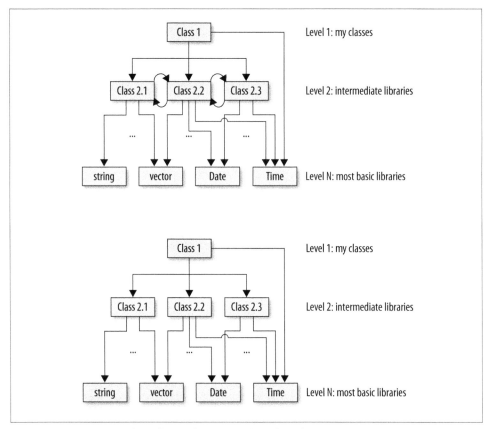

Figure 14-1. Application that allows references to the code in the same layers, versus one with a strict separation of layers

Each piece of code that expects some input must be tested with both correct and incorrect inputs. Try to "push" the code and see how it behaves not only under normal but also abnormal circumstances. For instance, if the code expects a pointer (or pointers) to some inputs, what would happen if you provide NULL(s) instead? If an algorithm expects integers, test whether there could be an integer overflow. If an algorithm expects doubles, test what happens if they are very small or very large. See how code behaves when different inputs differ by several orders of magnitude. Will the algorithm lose its accuracy?

If the algorithm works with input of a variable size (e.g., an array, vector, or matrix, or if the code reads several numbers from a file), see what happens when the size of input grows by an order of magnitude. You must have an understanding of the *complexity* of your algorithm, e.g., if the input contains N units of information, how much does the time of processing increase as a function of N when N increases? Then test it whether this is true in practice.

If the algorithm does some calculation numerically but in specific cases it has an analytical solution, compare them. If there is asymptotic behavior when some parameter becomes small or large, test it.

If the algorithm does something in a very smart and efficient way, consider writing a brute-force version of the same algorithm. Although this will be much slower, it will also be much simpler and therefore less error-prone. Then compare the results, at least for small input size.

If an algorithm takes as an input an arbitrary set of numbers, such as in the case of sorting, it is usually a good idea to generate test inputs in a pseudo-random manner—e.g., using the function `rand()`—so that you can create a lot of different test sets easily. This technique still allows the tests to be repeatable, because you can recreate the same set by specifying the same seed for the random number generator.

Always look for special cases. If the algorithm takes an array, what happens if it is empty or contains just one element? What if all elements of an array are the same? If it takes a matrix, what happens if the determinant of that matrix is zero?

If you use hash sets or hash maps, test them for collisions with a realistic set of inputs. Try to look for worst-case scenarios.

If your inputs depend on a calendar date, make sure to include the February 29th in a leap year. I have found that in algorithms generating sets of dates starting from some initial date, this is usually a very special case that can sometimes lead to the discovery of rare but interesting bugs. Therefore, if you are testing data that includes a range of dates, make sure that it is at least five years long so that it includes at least one leap year. (Strictly speaking, not every five-year interval includes a leap year, because the years 1900, 2100, 2200, and 2300 are not leap years, so you might need about nine years of data instead, depending on the century in which you are reading this book.)

Automate your testing as much as possible. The best set of tests is one that runs with one push of a button and tests everything there is to test about your code. There are many frameworks and utilities that make it easy to achieve this automation.

Plan your work so that you spend between 30% to 50% of your time testing. This is the part of planning that is very easy to underestimate and where things tend to go wrong, thus ruining delivery schedules. Remember: the more effort you spend on testing, the easier your life will be when your code goes into production.

CHAPTER 15

Debug-On-Error Strategy

By this time you probably have your program written and containing a lot of sanity checks, some permanent and some temporary. Now it is time to test it. Let's go bug hunting, one bug at a time. Our testing algorithm is very simple:

1. Run your code with sanity checks on, trying to cover all possible cases.
2. If any sanity check fails, fix the code and return to step 1.
3. If you've made it to step 3, you can be reasonably sure your code works correctly. Well done!

In my personal experience, this strategy makes testing a much faster, more efficient, and more enjoyable procedure than it would otherwise be, when your code does strange things and does not provide any explanation for its behavior. All you have to do to make this process effective is to insert enough sanity checks in your code while writing it and to make them as informative as possible. In short, the more sanity checks you have in your code, the more you can guarantee that it works correctly after it has passed all the checks.

Let's consider how the SCPP_TEST_ASSERT macro can be switched on. Take a closer look in the file *scpp_assert.hpp*, where it is defined:

```
#ifdef _DEBUG
#  define SCPP_TEST_ASSERT_ON
#endif

#ifdef SCPP_TEST_ASSERT_ON
#  define SCPP_TEST_ASSERT(condition,msg) SCPP_ASSERT(condition, msg)
#else
#  define SCPP_TEST_ASSERT(condition,msg) // do nothing
#endif
```

If you compile your project in debug mode, a symbol named _DEBUG is defined during compilation (this might be compiler-dependent, but it is definitely true for Microsoft Visual Studio). In this case, your sanity checks (e.g., the SCPP_TEST_ASSERT macro) are on. Our option for running the code are summarized in Table 15-1.

Table 15-1. Testing modes

Level	Purpose	Compilation mode	Test sanity checks
1	Testing with debugging on error	Debug	On
2	Fast testing	Release	On
3	Production	Release	Off

Options 1 and 3 are obvious enough: most of the time you will want to test your code while it is compiled in debug mode, and probably running it inside a debugger. However, if your program does a lot of number crunching, and if switching sanity checks on and compiling in the debug mode slow it down too much, you have option 2: testing the code compiled in release mode with sanity checks on. Not having the luxury of exploring the code in the debugger makes it especially important that your error messages contain enough information to allow you to fix the bug.

If your program is fast enough to run with sanity checks in debug mode, the easiest way to catch a bug is to open the *scpp_assert.cpp* file, find the comment "This is a good place to put your debug breakpoint:", and put a debug breakpoint on the next line (which can be the line starting with either `throw` or `cerr`, depending on how the code was compiled):

```
void SCPP_AssertErrorHandler(const char* file_name,
                unsigned line_number,
                const char* message) {
  // This is a good place to put your debug breakpoint:
  // You can also add writing of the same info into a log file if appropriate.

#ifdef SCPP_THROW_EXCEPTION_ON_BUG
  throw scpp::ScppAssertFailedException(file_name, line_number, message);
#else
  cerr << message << " in file " << file_name
       << " #" << line_number << endl << flush;
  // Terminate application
  exit(1);
#endif
```

This is the reason I created this error handler function. Simply knowing the filename and line number where the error occurred might not help you much. But if you put your debugger breakpoint there, the debugger will stop on it during every execution of this line, even if the bug occurs on only the 10th or even the 10,000th iteration. By putting the breakpoint *inside* the error handler function, you are guaranteed that your program will run to the first error and stop in the debugger, as shown in Figure 15-1.

If the text of the error message is not enough to figure out why the error happened, you can go up the call stack into the function where the error occurred and examine the variables to figure out what happened and why. On the other hand, if your debugger doesn't stop on this breakpoint, you should not be too disappointed—your program passed all sanity checks!

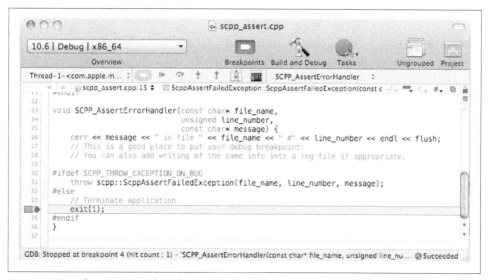

Figure 15-1. Debugger stopped inside the error handler function in XCode (Max OS X Leopard)

CHAPTER 16

Making Your Code Debugger-Friendly

Have you ever tried to look inside some object in the debugger and been frustrated that the debugger shows the details of the object's physical implementation instead of the logical information that the object is supposed to represent? Let me illustrate this using an example of a Date class that represents calendar dates, such as December 26, 2011. If you look into this object in the debugger, chances are you will not see anything resembling "December 26, 2011" or any human-readable information at all, but rather an integer that requires some decoding to convert into a date it represents.

It all depends on how the Date type is implemented. I have seen the following three implementations:

1.
```
class Date {
  // some code

  private:
    int day_, month_, year_;
```
2. `typedef Date int; // in YYYYMMDD format`
3.
```
class Date {
  // some code

  private:
    int number_of_days_; //  Number of calendar days since the "anchor date"
```

The first implementation is pretty self-evident and is a pleasure to debug. In the second case, the date December 26, 2011 is represented by an integer 20111226, which is also easily readable by a human once you know the formula behind it.

In the last case, the internal representation of a Date is the number of days that have passed since some arbitrarily chosen date far enough in the past, that the day represented by 1 is 1/1/1900 or 1/1/0000 or something of this sort.

While the first two implementations are very debugger-friendly, they have a serious problem. The Date type is supposed to support "date arithmetic," i.e., operations such as adding a number of days to a date, or calculating the number of days between two dates. In the cases of implementations 1 and 2 such number arithmetic is extremely slow, while in the case of implementation 3 it is as efficient as adding and subtracting integers.

For this reason, any serious implementation of Date uses approach 3. However, when you look at this Date object in the debugger, it is a pain to figure out what the actual calendar date is. For example, in the class Date we will consider momentarily, the date December 26, 2011 looks like 734497 in the debugger, and when you are working with code that contains a lot of dates—for example, some financial contract that pays quarterly for the next 30 years, and also has some additional dates a couple of days before each payment date relevant for calculation—debugging becomes a challenge.

But it doesn't have to be. The solution to this problem is to make the code of the class Date "debugger-friendly," meaning that when compiled in debug mode, it provides additional information in the debugger to represent the date in a human-readable form (either as "December 26, 2011" or at least 20111226). However, given that this additional functionality requires some calculations and increases the size of the object, I've decided to compromise and settle on the second solution, representing the debugging info of the date in YYYYMMDD format, i.e., as 20111226.

The complete source code for the class Date is provided in Appendix J in the *scpp_date.hpp* and *scpp_date.cpp* files. Here I just include snippets from these files that provide this additional debugging information. In the header file we find:

```
class Date {
 public:
   // some code

 private:
   int date_; // number of days from A.D., i.e. 01/01/0000 is 1.

#ifdef _DEBUG
   int yyyymmdd_;
#endif

 void SyncDebug() {
#ifdef _DEBUG
   yyyymmdd_ = AsYYYYMMDD();
#endif
 }

 void SyncDebug(unsigned year, unsigned month, unsigned day) {
#ifdef _DEBUG
   yyyymmdd_ = 10000*year + 100*month + day;
#endif
 }
};
```

First, the implementation is based on a number of days since some day in the past. In addition, when compiled in debug mode, the symbol _DEBUG is defined and the class has an additional data member int yyyymmdd_, which will contain the date in the YYYYMMDD format. To fill this data member out, there are two functions

SyncDebug(), so named because they synchronize the debug information with the actual date_ contained in the object. When compiled in release mode, these two functions do nothing, and in debug mode they update the yyyymmdd_ data member. These functions are called from every non-const method of the class after modifying the date_ data member, for example:

```
Date& operator ++ () {
  ++date_;
  SyncDebug();
  return *this;
}

// some other non-const methods

Date& operator += (int nDays) {
  date_ += nDays;
  SyncDebug();
  return *this;
}

// even more non-const methods
```

and also in a constructor:

```
Date::Date(unsigned year, unsigned month, unsigned day) {
  SCPP_TEST_ASSERT(year>=1900, "Year must be >=1900.")
  SCPP_TEST_ASSERT(JAN<=month && month<=DEC,
    "Wrong month " << month << " must be 1..12.")
#ifdef SCPP_TEST_ASSERT_ON
  unsigned ml = MonthLength(month, year);
  SCPP_TEST_ASSERT(1<=day && day<=ml,
    "Wrong day: " << day << " must be 1.." << ml << ".");
#endif
  int n_years_before = year - 1;
  date_ = 365*n_years_before + n_years_before/4 - n_years_before/100
        + n_years_before/400 + day + NumberOfDaysBeforeMonth(month, year);

  SyncDebug(year, month, day);
}
```

Figure 16-1 shows how the Date object looks in the XCode debugger as a result of all this additional activity in debug mode.

The variable d of type Date is shown in the upper right columns. In the "Arguments" column find d, and under it you can see its data members, while in the next column, "Values," you can see that:

- date_ is equal to 734497.
- yyyymmdd_ is equal to 20111226.

The presence of the latter value makes decoding the date in the object as easy as separating the last two pairs of digits from the first four.

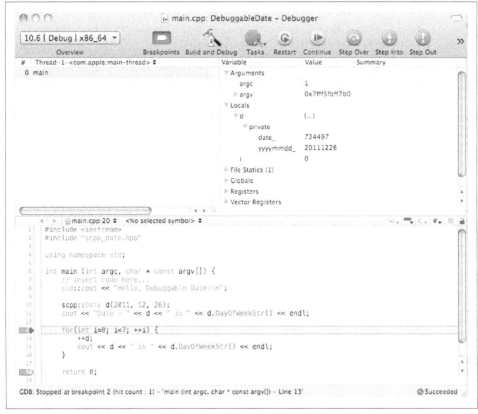

Figure 16-1. Looking at the "debuggable" Date object in the XCode debugger

The example of the Date class discussed here is just that: an example of an approach to making your class friendly to a debugger. I started to work on this mostly out of frustration when trying to look into STL containers in the debugger and finding a lot of interesting details about their implementation instead of what numbers or strings or other objects they actually contained. Making STL containers debugger-friendly on the level of code could be (and was) done, though it makes the code compiled in debug mode exceptionally slow. However, this problem was addressed recently on the level of the debugger: Microsoft Visual Studio 2010 shows the logical contents (as opposed to implementation details) of STL containers, such as a vector, set, or map (Figure 16-2).

Thus, there is hope that this idea will soon reach debuggers working under Unix, Linux, and Mac OS too.

In the case of a specific class you create, if its implementation differs from the logical information it represents, it is up to you to make it debugger-friendly. Usually it is not difficult, and you will be glad you did it as you debug your program.

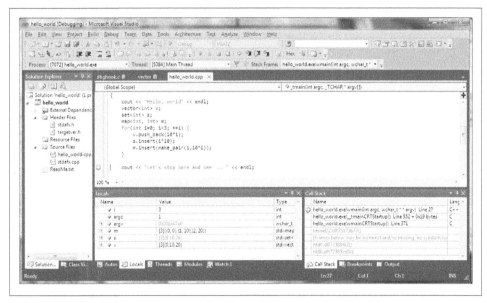

Figure 16-2. STL vector, set, and map in the Microsoft Visual Studio 2010 debugger

CHAPTER 17

Conclusion

Now that we've reached the end of this book, let's go back and summarize the guidelines and strategies we've discussed. The first guideline is that we want to diagnose as many errors at compile time as possible. All the other errors will be diagnosed at runtime, and most of the strategies in this book concentrate on catching these errors.

When catching errors at runtime, we are trying to achieve two contrasting goals:

- Testing as many sanity checks as possible.
- Having our code run as fast as possible in production.

This can be achieved by making some of the sanity checks temporary. To do this, you need to enable your checks to be switched on and off at compile time and activate them for testing only.

Here is a summary of all the rules formulated in this book.

For diagnosing errors at compile time (Chapter 2):

- Prohibit implicit type conversions: declare constructors taking one parameter with the `explicit` keyword and avoid conversion operators.
- Use different classes for different data types.
- Do not use `enums` to create `int` constants; use them to create new types.

To avoid an "index out of bounds" error (Chapter 4):

- Do not use static or dynamically allocated arrays; use a template array or vector instead.
- Do not use brackets on the `new` and `delete` operators; leave allocation of multiple elements to the template vector.
- Use `scpp:vector` instead of `std::vector`, and `scpp::array` instead of a static array. Switch the sanity checks on.

- For a two-dimensional array, use the `scpp::matrix` class (or similar classes for higher-dimension arrays) with `operator ()` providing indexes-out-of-bounds checks.

To avoid errors in pointer arithmetic (Chapter 5):

- Avoid using pointer arithmetic at all. Use a template vector or array with an index instead.

To avoid errors with invalid pointers, references, and iterators (Chapter 6):

- Do not hold pointers, references, or iterators to the element of a container after you've modified the container.

To avoid uninitialized variables, especially data members of a class (Chapter 7):

- Do not use built-in types such as `int`, `unsigned`, `double`, `bool`, etc., for class data members; instead use `Int`, `Unsigned`, `Double`, `Bool`, etc. You will not need to initialize them in constructors.
- If you use these classes instead of built-in types for passing parameters to functions, you get additional type safety.

To avoid memory leaks (Chapter 8):

- Every time you create an object using the `new` operator, immediately assign the result to a smart pointer (a reference counting pointer or scoped pointer is recommended).
- Use the new operator only without brackets. If you need to create an array, create a new template vector, which is a single object.
- Avoid circular references.
- When writing a function that returns a pointer, return a corresponding smart pointer instead of a raw one, to enforce the ownership of the result.

To catch dereferencing a NULL pointer at runtime (Chapter 9):

- If you have a pointer that owns the object it points to, use a smart pointer (a reference-counting pointer or scoped pointer).
- When you have a raw pointer T* that points to an object you do not own, use the template class `Ptr<T>` instead.
- For a `const` pointer (e.g., `const T*`) use `Ptr<const T>`.

To avoid errors in copy-constructors and assignment operators (Chapter 10):

- Whenever possible, avoid writing copy constructor and assignment operators for your classes.
- If the default versions created for you automatically by the compiler do not work for you, consider prohibiting copying instances of your class by declaring the copy constructor and assignment operator private.

To avoid problems when throwing exceptions from constructors (Chapter 11):

- Design your class in such a way that the destructor is empty.

To avoid errors when writing comparison operators (Chapter 12):

- Write a `CompareTo()` function and use the `SCPP_DEFINE_COMPARISON_OPERATORS` macro to implement all six comparison operators for your class.

To avoid errors when calling C-library functions such as buffer overflows and crashes caused by NULL pointers (Chapter 13):

- Avoid using C string libraries; use the `string` and `ostringstream` C++ classes instead.

The best possible testing mode is to compile code in debug mode with all sanity checks activated. In this mode, all runtime errors will lead to calls to the same error handler function where you can wait with a debug breakpoint. The code will run until a sanity check fails, at which time you will have an opportunity to debug the code that leads to the failure.

The next best mode is slightly faster: running tests when code is compiled in release mode with sanity checks on and relying on the completeness of the error messages to diagnose the errors. This mode might be necessary if the code compiled in debug mode with sanity checks on is too slow. You might even want to leave some of the sanity checks on in production if you think they might be triggered. For this reason, I've made writing these sanity checks as easy as possible, so you can write as many of them as you need and make them informative enough to diagnose the error without the use of a debugger.

Finally, when your tests pass all your sanity checks, you have good reason to believe that your program is working correctly. And the more sanity checks you've put in there, the more reason you have to believe this is true.

If you follow all the rules in this book, you will essentially be using a "safer" subset of C++ that should lower the "bug count" in your code. Of course, this book covers only the most common errors one can make when programming in C++, so even if you do follow all the rules, there is still lots of opportunity for mistakes. Therefore, instead of being titled *Safe C++*, this book could have been more realistically called *Safer C++*. Of course, completely safe C++ (or any other language) is an unattainable dream, but I hope that avoiding the errors discussed in this book brings us one step closer to this goal.

The strategy discussed in this book looks very simple. That's because it is. The whole idea of this book can be summarized as follows: *design your code to be self-diagnosing.* This strategy makes testing faster, easier, less stressful, and more productive; it relies on the compiler and runtime code to catch your errors, it speeds up development, makes testing much less stressful and more productive, and at the end of the day makes your code more reliable. Go ahead and apply it to your next project—I think you'll agree with me that it works!

Source Code for the scpp Library Used in This Book

Although you will download this library from my website at *https://github.com/vladimir -kushnir/SafeCPlusPlus* for use in your projects, I'm including it here so you can check it at your convenience while reading the book.

Source Code for the files
scpp_assert.hpp and scpp_assert.cpp

File *scpp_assert.hpp*

```cpp
#ifndef __SCPP_ASSERT_HPP_INCLUDED__
#define __SCPP_ASSERT_HPP_INCLUDED__

#include <sstream> // ostringstream

#ifdef SCPP_THROW_EXCEPTION_ON_BUG
#include <exception>

namespace scpp {
// This exception is thrown when the sanity checks defined below fail,
// and #ifdef SCPP_THROW_EXCEPTION_ON_BUG.
class ScppAssertFailedException : public std::exception {
 public:
   ScppAssertFailedException(const char* file_name,
                 unsigned line_number,
                 const char* message);

   virtual const char* what() const throw () { return what_.c_str(); }

   virtual ~ScppAssertFailedException() throw () {}
 private:
   std::string what_;
};
} // namespace scpp
#endif

void SCPP_AssertErrorHandler(const char* file_name,
                 unsigned line_number,
                 const char* message);

// Permanent sanity check macro.
#define SCPP_ASSERT(condition, msg)                \
    if(!(condition)) {                             \
        std::ostringstream s;                      \
```

```
              s << msg;                                    \
              SCPP_AssertErrorHandler(                      \
                  __FILE__, __LINE__, s.str().c_str() );   \
      }

   #ifdef _DEBUG
   #  define SCPP_TEST_ASSERT_ON
   #endif

   // Temporary (for testing only) sanity check macro
   #ifdef SCPP_TEST_ASSERT_ON
   #  define SCPP_TEST_ASSERT(condition,msg) SCPP_ASSERT(condition, msg)
   #else
   #  define SCPP_TEST_ASSERT(condition,msg) // do nothing
   #endif

   #endif // __SCPP_ASSERT_HPP_INCLUDED__
```

File *scpp_assert.cpp*

```cpp
   #include "scpp_assert.hpp"

   #include <iostream>  // cerr, endl, flush
   #include <stdlib.h>  // exit()


   using namespace std;

   #ifdef SCPP_THROW_EXCEPTION_ON_BUG
   namespace scpp {
     ScppAssertFailedException::ScppAssertFailedException(const char* file_name,
                               unsigned line_number,
                               const char* message) {
       ostringstream s;
       s << "SCPP assertion failed with message '" << message
         << "' in file " << file_name << " #" << line_number;

       what_ = s.str();
     }
   }
   #endif

   void SCPP_AssertErrorHandler(const char* file_name,
                    unsigned line_number,
                    const char* message) {
     // This is a good place to put your debug breakpoint:
     // You can also add writing of the same info into a log file if appropriate.

   #ifdef SCPP_THROW_EXCEPTION_ON_BUG
     throw scpp::ScppAssertFailedException(file_name, line_number, message);
   #else
     cerr << message << " in file " << file_name << " #" << line_number << endl << flush;
     // Terminate application
     exit(1);
   #endif
   }
```

Source Code for the file scpp_vector.hpp

```cpp
#ifndef __SCPP_VECTOR_HPP_INCLUDED__
#define __SCPP_VECTOR_HPP_INCLUDED__

#include <vector>
#include "scpp_assert.hpp"


namespace scpp {

// Wrapper around std::vector, has temporary sanity checks in the operators [].
template <typename T>
class vector : public std::vector<T> {
 public:
  typedef unsigned size_type;

  // Most commonly used constructors:
  explicit vector( size_type n = 0  )
  : std::vector<T>(n)
  {}

  vector( size_type n, const T& value )
  : std::vector<T>(n, value)
  {}

  template <class InputIterator> vector ( InputIterator first, InputIterator last )
  : std::vector<T>(first, last)
  {}

  // Note: we do not provide a copy-ctor and assignment operator.
  // we rely on default versions of these methods generated by the compiler.

  T& operator [] (size_type index) {
    SCPP_TEST_ASSERT(index < std::vector<T>::size(),
      "Index " << index << " must be less than "
      << std::vector<T>::size());
    return std::vector<T>::operator[](index);
```

```
      }
      const T& operator [] (size_type index) const {
        SCPP_TEST_ASSERT(index < std::vector<T>::size(),
          "Index " << index << " must be less than "
          << std::vector<T>::size());
        return std::vector<T>::operator[](index);
      }
    };
} // namespace scpp


template <typename T>
inline
std::ostream& operator << (std::ostream& os, const scpp::vector<T>& v) {
  for(unsigned i=0; i<v.size(); ++i) {
    os << v[i];
    if( i + 1 < v.size() )
      os << " ";
  }
  return os;
}

#endif // __SCPP_VECTOR_HPP_INCLUDED__
```

Source Code for the file scpp_array.hpp

```cpp
#ifndef __SCPP_ARRAY_HPP_INCLUDED__
#define __SCPP_ARRAY_HPP_INCLUDED__

#include "scpp_assert.hpp"

namespace scpp {

// Fixed-size array
template <typename T, unsigned N>
class array {
 public:
  typedef unsigned size_type;

  // Most commonly used constructors:
  array() {}
  explicit array(const T& initial_value) {
    for(size_type i=0; i<size(); ++i)
      data_[i] = initial_value;
  }

  size_type size() const { return N; }

  // Note: we do not provide a copy-ctor and assignment operator.
  // we rely on default versions of these methods generated by the compiler.

  T& operator [] (size_type index) {
    SCPP_TEST_ASSERT(index < N,
      "Index " << index << " must be less than " << N);
    return data_[index];
  }

  const T& operator [] (size_type index) const {
    SCPP_TEST_ASSERT(index < N,
      "Index " << index << " must be less than " << N);
    return data_[index];
  }

  // Accessors
  T* begin() { return &data_[0]; }
```

```
  const T* begin() const { return &data_[0]; }

  // Returns pointer PAST the end of the array.
  T* end() { return &data_[N]; }
  const T* end() const { return &data_[N]; }

  private:
  T data_[N];
};
} // namespace scpp


template <typename T, unsigned N>
inline
std::ostream& operator << (std::ostream& os, const scpp::array<T,N>& a) {
  for( unsigned i=0; i<a.size(); ++i ) {
    os << a[i];
    if( i + 1 < a.size() )
        os << " ";
  }
  return os;
}

#endif // __SCPP_ARRAY_HPP_INCLUDED__
```

Source Code for the file scpp_matrix.hpp

```cpp
#ifndef __SCPP_MATRIX_HPP_INCLUDED__
#define __SCPP_MATRIX_HPP_INCLUDED__

#include <ostream>
#include <vector>

#include "scpp_assert.hpp"

namespace scpp {

// Two-dimensional rectangular matrix.
template <typename T>
class matrix {
  public:
  typedef unsigned size_type;

  matrix(size_type num_rows, size_type num_cols)
    : rows_(num_rows), cols_(num_cols), data_(num_rows * num_cols)
  {
    SCPP_TEST_ASSERT(num_rows > 0,
      "Number of rows in a matrix must be positive");
    SCPP_TEST_ASSERT(num_cols > 0,
      "Number of columns in a matrix must be positive");
  }

  matrix(size_type num_rows, size_type num_cols, const T& init_value)
    : rows_(num_rows), cols_(num_cols), data_(num_rows * num_cols, init_value)
  {
    SCPP_TEST_ASSERT(num_rows > 0, "Number of rows in a matrix must be positive");
    SCPP_TEST_ASSERT(num_cols > 0, "Number of columns in a matrix must be positive");
  }

  size_type num_rows() const { return rows_; }
  size_type num_cols() const { return cols_; }

  // Accessors: return element by row and column.
```

```cpp
    T& operator() ( size_type row, size_type col )
    {
      return data_[ index( row, col ) ];
    }

    const T& operator() ( size_type row, size_type col ) const
    {
      return data_[ index( row, col ) ];
    }

    private:
    size_type rows_, cols_;
    std::vector<T> data_;

    size_type index(size_type row, size_type col) const {
      SCPP_TEST_ASSERT(row < rows_, "Row " << row  << " must be less than " << rows_);
       SCPP_TEST_ASSERT(col < cols_, "Column " << col  << " must be less than " << cols_);
      return cols_ * row + col;
    }
};

}  // namespace scpp

template <typename T>
inline
std::ostream& operator << (std::ostream& os, const scpp::matrix<T>& m) {
  for( unsigned r =0; r<m.num_rows(); ++r ) {
    for( unsigned c=0; c<m.num_cols(); ++c ) {
      os << m(r,c);
      if( c + 1 < m.num_cols() )
        os << "\t";
    }
    os << "\n";
  }
  return os;
}

#endif // __SCPP_MATRIX_HPP_INCLUDED__
```

Source Code for the file scpp_types.hpp

```cpp
#ifndef __SCPP_TYPES_HPP_INCLUDED__
#define __SCPP_TYPES_HPP_INCLUDED__

#include <ostream>
#include "scpp_assert.hpp"

// Template wrapper around a built-in type T.
// Behaves exactly as T, except initialized by default to 0.
template<typename T>
class TNumber {
public:
  TNumber(const T& x=0)
    : data_(x) {
  }

  operator T () const { return data_; }

  TNumber& operator = (const T& x) {
    data_ = x;
    return *this;
  }

  // postfix operator x++
  TNumber operator ++ (int) {
    TNumber<T> copy(*this);
    ++data_;
    return copy;
  }

  // prefix operator ++x
  TNumber& operator ++ () {
    ++data_;
    return *this;
  }

  TNumber& operator += (T x) {
```

```cpp
      data_ += x;
      return *this;
    }

    TNumber& operator -= (T x) {
      data_ -= x;
      return *this;
    }

    TNumber& operator *= (T x) {
      data_ *= x;
      return *this;
    }

    TNumber& operator /= (T x) {
      SCPP_TEST_ASSERT(x!=0, "Attempt to divide by 0");
      data_ /= x;
      return *this;
    }

    T operator / (T x)
    {
      SCPP_TEST_ASSERT(x!=0, "Attempt to divide by 0");
      return data_ / x;
    }
private:
  T data_;
};

typedef long long int64;
typedef unsigned long long unsigned64;

typedef    TNumber<int>      Int;
typedef    TNumber<unsigned>    Unsigned;
typedef    TNumber<int64>    Int64;
typedef    TNumber<unsigned64> Unsigned64;
typedef    TNumber<float>    Float;
typedef    TNumber<double>    Double;
typedef    TNumber<char>    Char;

class Bool {
public:
  Bool(bool x=false)
    : data_(x)
  {}

  operator bool () const { return data_; }
  Bool& operator = (bool x) {
    data_ = x;
    return *this;
  }

  Bool& operator &= (bool x) {
    data_ &= x;
```

```cpp
    return *this;
  }

  Bool& operator |= (bool x) {
    data_ |= x;
    return *this;
  }

private:
  bool data_;
};

inline
std::ostream& operator << (std::ostream& os, Bool b) {
  if(b)
    os << "True";
  else
    os << "False";
  return os;
}

#define SCPP_DEFINE_COMPARISON_OPERATORS(Class) \
  bool operator < (const Class& that) const { return CompareTo(that) < 0; } \
  bool operator > (const Class& that) const { return CompareTo(that) > 0; } \
  bool operator ==(const Class& that) const { return CompareTo(that) ==0; } \
  bool operator <=(const Class& that) const { return CompareTo(that) <=0; } \
  bool operator >=(const Class& that) const { return CompareTo(that) >=0; } \
  bool operator !=(const Class& that) const { return CompareTo(that) !=0; }


#endif // __SCPP_TYPES_HPP_INCLUDED__
```

Source Code for the file
scpp_refcountptr.hpp

```cpp
#ifndef __SCPP_REFCOUNTPTR_HPP_INCLUDED__
#define __SCPP_REFCOUNTPTR_HPP_INCLUDED__

#include "scpp_assert.hpp"

namespace scpp {

// Reference-counting pointer.  Takes ownership of an object.  Can be copied.
template <typename T>
class RefCountPtr {
  public:

  explicit RefCountPtr(T* p = NULL) {
    Create(p);
  }

  RefCountPtr(const RefCountPtr<T>& rhs) {
    Copy(rhs);
  }

  RefCountPtr<T>& operator=(const RefCountPtr<T>& rhs) {
    if(ptr_ != rhs.ptr_) {
      Kill();
      Copy(rhs);
    }

    return *this;
  }

  RefCountPtr<T>& operator=(T* p) {
    if(ptr_ != p) {
      Kill();
      Create(p);
    }

    return *this;
```

```cpp
    }

    ~RefCountPtr() {
      Kill();
    }

    T* Get() const { return ptr_; }

    T* operator->() const {
      SCPP_TEST_ASSERT(ptr_ != NULL, "Attempt to use operator -> on NULL pointer.");
      return ptr_;
    }

    T& operator* () const {
      SCPP_TEST_ASSERT(ptr_ != NULL, "Attempt to use operator * on NULL pointer.");
      return *ptr_;
    }

private:
    T*   ptr_;
    int*  count_;

    void Create(T* p) {
      ptr_ = p;
      if(ptr_ != NULL) {
        count_ = new int;
        *count_ = 1;
      } else {
        count_ = NULL;
      }
    }

    void Copy(const RefCountPtr<T>& rhs) {
      ptr_ = rhs.ptr_;
      count_ = rhs.count_;
      if(count_ != NULL)
        ++(*count_);
    }

    void Kill() {
      if(count_ != NULL) {
        if(--(*count_) == 0) {
          delete ptr_;
          delete count_;
        }
      }
    }

};
} // namespace scpp

#endif // __SCPP_REFCOUNTPTR_HPP_INCLUDED__
```

Source Code for the file scpp_scopedptr.hpp

```cpp
#ifndef __SCPP_SCOPEDPTR_HPP_INCLUDED__
#define __SCPP_SCOPEDPTR_HPP_INCLUDED__

#include "scpp_assert.hpp"

namespace scpp {

// Scoped pointer, takes ownership of an object, could not be copied.
template <typename T>
class ScopedPtr {
  public:

  explicit ScopedPtr(T* p = NULL)
  : ptr_(p) {
  }

  ScopedPtr<T>& operator=(T* p) {
    if(ptr_ != p)
    {
      delete ptr_;
      ptr_ = p;
    }

    return *this;
  }

  ~ScopedPtr() {
    delete ptr_;
  }

  T* Get() const {
    return ptr_;
  }

  T* operator->() const
  {
```

```cpp
    SCPP_TEST_ASSERT(ptr_ != NULL, "Attempt to use operator -> on NULL pointer.");
    return ptr_;
  }

  T& operator* () const {
    SCPP_TEST_ASSERT(ptr_ != NULL, "Attempt to use operator * on NULL pointer.");
    return *ptr_;
  }

  // Release ownership of the object to the caller.
  T* Release() {
    T* p = ptr_;
    ptr_ = NULL;
    return p;
  }

private:
  T*  ptr_;

  // Copy is prohibited:
  ScopedPtr(const ScopedPtr<T>& rhs);
  ScopedPtr<T>& operator=(const ScopedPtr<T>& rhs);
};

} // namespace scpp

#endif // __SCPP_SCOPEDPTR_HPP_INCLUDED__
```

Source Code for the file scpp_ptr.hpp

```cpp
#ifndef __SCPP_PTR_HPP_INCLUDED__
#define __SCPP_PTR_HPP_INCLUDED__

#include "scpp_assert.hpp"

namespace scpp {

// Template pointer, does not take ownership of an object.
template <typename T>
class Ptr {
  public:

  explicit Ptr(T* p = NULL)
  : ptr_(p) {
  }

  T* Get() const {
    return ptr_;
  }

  Ptr<T>& operator=(T* p) {
    ptr_ = p;
    return *this;
  }

  T* operator->() const {
    SCPP_TEST_ASSERT(ptr_ != NULL, "Attempt to use operator -> on NULL pointer.");
    return ptr_;
  }

  T& operator* () const {
    SCPP_TEST_ASSERT(ptr_ != NULL, "Attempt to use operator * on NULL pointer.");
    return *ptr_;
  }

private:
  T*  ptr_;
};
```

```
} // namespace scpp

#endif // __SCPP_PTR_HPP_INCLUDED__
```

Source Code for the file scpp_date.hpp and scpp_date.cpp

File ***scpp_date.hpp***

```cpp
#ifndef __SCPP_DATE_HPP_INCLUDED__
#define __SCPP_DATE_HPP_INCLUDED__

#include <iostream>
#include <string>

#include "scpp_assert.hpp"
#include "scpp_types.hpp"

/*
  Date class.
  Features:
    All date arithmetic operators and comparisons are provided.
    Date arithmetic is implemented as an integer arithmetic.
    No Y2K problems -- all years must be >= 1900.
    Default output format is American (MM/DD/YYYY).
    In debug one can see the date in debugger as yyyymmdd --
      just point your debugger to a yyyymmdd_ data member.

  No implicit type conversions are allowed.

*/
namespace scpp {
class Date {
public:
  // Creates an empty (invalid in terms of IsValid()) date.
  Date();

  // Input format: "mm/dd/yyyy".
  explicit Date(const char* str_date);

  // Same as above.
  explicit Date(const std::string& str_date);
```

```cpp
// Date from integer in the YYYYMMDD format, e.g. Dec. 26, 2011 is 20111226.
explicit Date(unsigned yyyymmdd);

// Year must be 4-digit,
// month is 1-based, i.e. 1 .. 12,
// day is 1 .. MonthLength() <= 31
Date(unsigned year, unsigned month, unsigned day);

// Returns true if the date is not empty,
// as is the case when it is created by the default constructor.
// Most operations on invalid date are not allowed
// (will call error handler).
bool IsValid() const { return date_!=0; }

// Returns date in YYYYMMDD format, e.g. Dec. 26, 2011 is 20111226.
unsigned AsYYYYMMDD() const;

// 4-digit year.
unsigned Year() const;

enum { JAN=1, FEB, MAR, APR, MAY, JUN, JUL, AUG, SEP, OCT, NOV, DEC };
// Returns month number JAN .. DEC, i.e. 1..12.
unsigned Month() const;

// Day of month 1 .. MonthLength() <= 31.
unsigned DayOfMonth() const;

static bool IsLeap(unsigned year);

typedef enum { SUN, MON, TUE, WED, THU, FRI, SAT } DayOfWeekType;
// Returns day of week SUN .. SAT.
DayOfWeekType DayOfWeek() const;

// "Sunday", "Monday" .. "Saturday".
const char* DayOfWeekStr() const;

int Data() const { return date_; }

typedef enum { FRMT_AMERICAN,   // MM/DD/YYYY
               FRMT_EUROPEAN  // MM.DD.YYYY
               // one can add formats in here if necessary.
    } DateOutputFormat;

enum { MIN_BUFFER_SIZE=11 };
// The function prints a date into a user-provided buffer
// and returns the same buffer.
// Make sure the buffer size >= MIN_BUFFER_SIZE chars at least.
char* AsString(char* buffer, unsigned bufLen,
               DateOutputFormat frmt=FRMT_AMERICAN) const;

// Same as above, but C++ style.
std::string AsString(DateOutputFormat frmt=FRMT_AMERICAN) const;

// Returns negative int, 0 or positive int in cases of *this<d, *this==d and *this>d.
int CompareTo(const Date& d) const {
```

```cpp
    SCPP_TEST_ASSERT(IsValid(), "Date is not valid")
    SCPP_TEST_ASSERT(d.IsValid(), "Date is not valid")

    return date_ - d.date_;
  }

    SCPP_DEFINE_COMPARISON_OPERATORS(Date)

  Date& operator ++ () {
    ++date_;
    SyncDebug();
    return *this;
  }

  Date operator ++ (int) {
    Date copy(*this);
    ++(*this);
    return copy;
  }

  Date& operator -- () {
    --date_;
    SyncDebug();
    return *this;
  }

  Date operator -- (int) {
    Date copy(*this);
    --(*this);
    return copy;
  }

  Date& operator += (int nDays) {
    date_ += nDays;
    SyncDebug();
    return *this;
  }

  Date& operator -= (int nDays) {
    (*this) += (-nDays);
    return *this;
  }

private:
  int date_; // number of days from A.D., i.e. 01/01/0001 is 1.

#ifdef _DEBUG
  int yyyymmdd_;
#endif

  void SyncDebug() {
#ifdef _DEBUG
    yyyymmdd_ = AsYYYYMMDD();
#endif
  }
```

```
    void SyncDebug(unsigned year, unsigned month, unsigned day) {
#ifdef _DEBUG
      yyyymmdd_ = 10000*year + 100*month + day;
#endif
    }

    // Returns month's length in days,
    // input: month = 1 .. 12
    static unsigned MonthLength(unsigned month, unsigned year);

    // Returns number of calendar days before beginning of the month,
    // e.g. for JAN - 0,
    //      for FEB - 31,
    //      for MAR - 59 or 60 depending on the leap year.
    static unsigned NumberOfDaysBeforeMonth(unsigned month, unsigned year);
};
} // namespace scpp

inline std::ostream& operator<<(std::ostream& os, const scpp::Date& d) {
  char buffer[scpp::Date::MIN_BUFFER_SIZE];
  os << d.AsString(buffer, scpp::Date::MIN_BUFFER_SIZE);
  return os;
}

inline scpp::Date operator + (const scpp::Date& d, int nDays) {
  scpp::Date copy(d);
  return (copy += nDays);
}

inline scpp::Date operator - (const scpp::Date& d, int nDays) {
  scpp::Date copy(d);
  return (copy -= nDays);
}

inline int operator - (const scpp::Date& lhs, const scpp::Date& rhs) {
  return lhs.Data() - rhs.Data();
}
#endif // __SCPP_DATE_HPP_INCLUDED__
```

File *scpp_date.cpp*

```
#include "scpp_date.hpp"

#include <string.h>  // strlen
#include <stdlib.h>  // atoi

namespace scpp {
Date::Date()
: date_(0)
{
#ifdef _DEBUG
  yyyymmdd_ = 0;
#endif
```

```
}

Date::Date(const char* str_date) {
  SCPP_ASSERT(str_date!=NULL, "Date(): string argument=0.")

  // must be mm/dd/yyyy, at least m/d/yyyy
  SCPP_TEST_ASSERT(strlen(str_date)>=8, "Bad Date input: '" << str_date << "'.")

  unsigned mm, dd=0, yyyy=0;

  mm = atoi(str_date);
  for(const char* p=str_date; (*p)!='\0'; ++p) {
    if(*p=='/') {
      if(dd==0)
        dd = atoi(p+1);
      else {
        yyyy = atoi(p+1);
        break;
      }
    }
  }

  SCPP_TEST_ASSERT(mm!=0 && dd!=0 && yyyy!=0, "Bad Date input '" << str_date << "',
  must be MM/DD/YYYY.");

  *this = Date(yyyy, mm, dd);
}

Date::Date(const std::string& str) {
  *this = Date(str.c_str());
}

Date::Date(unsigned yyyymmdd) {
  int yyyy = yyyymmdd / 10000;
  int mmdd = yyyymmdd - 10000 * yyyy;
  int mm = mmdd / 100;
  int dd = mmdd - 100 * mm;

  *this = Date(yyyy, mm, dd);
}

Date::Date(unsigned year, unsigned month, unsigned day) {
  SCPP_TEST_ASSERT(year>=1900, "Year must be >=1900.")
  SCPP_TEST_ASSERT(JAN<=month && month<=DEC, "Wrong month " << month << " must be 1..12.")
#ifdef SCPP_TEST_ASSERT_ON
  unsigned ml = MonthLength(month, year);
  SCPP_TEST_ASSERT(1<=day && day<=ml, "Wrong day: " << day << " must be 1.." << ml << ".");
#endif
  int n_years_before = year-1;
  date_ = 365*n_years_before
    + n_years_before/4 - n_years_before/100 + n_years_before/400
    + day + NumberOfDaysBeforeMonth(month, year);

  SyncDebug(year, month, day);
}
```

```
unsigned Date::AsYYYYMMDD() const {
  unsigned y = Year();
  unsigned m = Month();
  unsigned d = Data() - Date(y, m, 1).Data() + 1;

  return y*10000 + m*100 + d;
}

bool Date::IsLeap(unsigned year) {
  if(year%4)
    return false;

  if(year%400 == 0)
    return true;

  if(year%100 == 0)
    return false;

  return true;
}

Date::DayOfWeekType Date::DayOfWeek() const {
  return (DayOfWeekType)(date_ % 7);
}

const char* Date::DayOfWeekStr() const {
  static const char* str_day_of_week[] = {
    "Sunday", "Monday", "Tuesday", "Wednesday",
    "Thursday", "Friday", "Saturday" };

  DayOfWeekType dow = DayOfWeek();
  return str_day_of_week[(unsigned)dow];
}

// static
unsigned Date::MonthLength(unsigned month, unsigned year) {
  static int month_length[13] = { 0, 31,28,31,30,31,30,31,31,30,31,30,31 };
  SCPP_TEST_ASSERT(year>=1900, "Wrong year: " << year << ", must be >=1900.");
  SCPP_TEST_ASSERT(JAN <= month && month <= DEC, "Wrong month " << month);
  if(month == FEB && IsLeap(year))
    return 29;
  return month_length[month];
}

// static
unsigned Date::NumberOfDaysBeforeMonth(unsigned month, unsigned year) {
  static int days_before_month[12] = { 0, 31,59,90,120,151,181,212,243,273,304,334 };
  SCPP_TEST_ASSERT(year>=1900, "Wrong year: " << year << ", must be >=1900.");
  SCPP_TEST_ASSERT(JAN <= month && month <= DEC, "Wrong month " << month);
  unsigned days_before = days_before_month[month - 1];
  if (month >= MAR && IsLeap(year))
    ++days_before;
  return days_before;
}
```

```cpp
unsigned Date::Year() const {
  SCPP_TEST_ASSERT(IsValid(), "Date is not valid")

  unsigned y = Data() / 365;
  while(Date(y,1,1).Data() > Data())
    --y;
  return y;
}

unsigned Date::Month() const {
  SCPP_TEST_ASSERT(IsValid(), "Date is not valid")

  unsigned y = Year();
  Date endOfLastYear(y-1, DEC, 31);
  unsigned day = Data() - endOfLastYear.Data();
  for(unsigned m=JAN; m<=DEC; ++m)
  {
    unsigned ml = MonthLength(m, y);
    if(day <= ml)
      return m;
    day -= ml;
  }
  SCPP_ASSERT(false, "Fatal algorith error.")
  return 0;
}

unsigned Date::DayOfMonth() const {
  SCPP_TEST_ASSERT(IsValid(), "Date is not valid")

  unsigned y = Year();
  unsigned m = Month();
  unsigned d = Data() - Date(y, m, 1).Data() + 1;
  SCPP_TEST_ASSERT(d > 0 && d <= MonthLength(m,y),
    "Wrong day " << d << " of month " << m << " year " << y );
  return d;
}

char* Date::AsString(char* buffer,  unsigned bufLen, DateOutputFormat frmt) const {
  SCPP_TEST_ASSERT(IsValid(), "Date is not valid")
  SCPP_TEST_ASSERT(bufLen>=MIN_BUFFER_SIZE,
    "Buffer is too short: " << bufLen << " must be at least " << MIN_BUFFER_SIZE)

  unsigned y = Year();
  unsigned m = Month();
  unsigned d = Data() - Date(y, m, 1).Data() + 1;

  switch(frmt) {
    case FRMT_AMERICAN:
      sprintf(buffer, "%02d/%02d/%04d", m, d, y);
      break;

    case FRMT_EUROPEAN:
      sprintf(buffer, "%02d.%02d.%4d", m, d, y);
      break;
```

```
        default:
            SCPP_ASSERT(false, "Wrong output format " << frmt);
    }

    return buffer;
}

std::string Date::AsString(DateOutputFormat frmt) const {
    char buffer[ 12 ];
    return AsString(buffer, sizeof(buffer), frmt);
}
} // namespace scpp
```

Index

We'd like to hear your suggestions for improving our indexes. Send email to *index@oreilly.com*.

V

Variant class, 6, 9

vectors

    adding too many elements to, 33–34

    pointers, references, iterators pointing to
           elements of, 33–34

    template vector, 21–22, 24–26

Visual Studio

    diagnosis of index-out-of-bounds errors by,
           26

    STL containers in debugger, 82

About the Author

Vladimir Kushnir obtained his Ph.D. in physics at the Institute for Solid State Physics, Academy of Sciences of the USSR. Since that time, Vladimir worked as an experimental physicist, using FORTRAN, C, and then C++, while working at Northwestern University and later at the Argonne National Laboratory. He then went to work with Wall Street firms, focusing mostly on calculations called "financial analytics," and having special interest in taking a calculation and making it run faster, sometimes by an order of magnitude. He lives with his wife Daria in Connecticut and when not programming in C++, enjoys jazz music and underwater photography in his spare time.

Colophon

The animal on the cover of *Safe C++* is the merlin (*Falcon columbarius*). Formerly known as the pigeon hawk, this bird was embraced for falconry among royalty in medieval Europe, especially by noble women—Mary Queen of Scots and Catherine the Great, in particular. There are various subspecies of the merlin, and it could be argued that there are two distinct variants: the North American merlin and the European merlin (*Falcon aesalon*).

This species is found at high latitudes all over North America in various habitats, including marshes, open woodland, and prairies. Merlins are migratory and, depending on the variant, will travel as far as South America and North Africa for winter months.

Merlins are lean, yet robust, birds of prey. Females are usually larger than males, growing up to nearly a foot in length with a wingspan of at least 20 inches. While female birds carry dark brown plumage, males usually have blue-gray colored feathers. Both have long, banded tails.

The merlin is an aggressive predator; as an aerial forager, it relies on agility and speed for its hunts. When in pursuit of a meal, merlins will often fly very low to the ground and use their surroundings to take their prey by surprise. They are also apt to capture prey midair. Its diet consists of smaller birds, such as sandpipers and the meadow pipit, as well as other small mammals and large insects.

Merlins are resourceful creatures; instead of building their own nests, they roost in old nests of other birds, like magpies or crows. They are also monogamous animals, and are known to demonstrate acrobatic displays of courtship. In fact, paired merlins will hunt cooperatively, with one bird flushing the prey toward its mate.

The cover image is from Johnson's *Natural History*. The cover font is Adobe ITC Garamond. The text font is Linotype Birka; the heading font is Adobe Myriad Condensed; and the code font is LucasFont's TheSansMonoCondensed.

Get even more for your money.

Join the O'Reilly Community, and register the O'Reilly books you own. It's free, and you'll get:

- $4.99 ebook upgrade offer
- 40% upgrade offer on O'Reilly print books
- Membership discounts on books and events
- Free lifetime updates to ebooks and videos
- Multiple ebook formats, DRM FREE
- Participation in the O'Reilly community
- Newsletters
- Account management
- 100% Satisfaction Guarantee

Signing up is easy:

1. Go to: oreilly.com/go/register
2. Create an O'Reilly login.
3. Provide your address.
4. Register your books.

Note: English-language books only

To order books online:
oreilly.com/store

For questions about products or an order:
orders@oreilly.com

To sign up to get topic-specific email announcements and/or news about upcoming books, conferences, special offers, and new technologies:
elists@oreilly.com

For technical questions about book content:
booktech@oreilly.com

To submit new book proposals to our editors:
proposals@oreilly.com

O'Reilly books are available in multiple DRM-free ebook formats. For more information:
oreilly.com/ebooks

Spreading the knowledge of innovators   oreilly.com

Have it your way.

Milton Keynes UK
Ingram Content Group UK Ltd.
UKHW031810111223
434184UK00010B/757